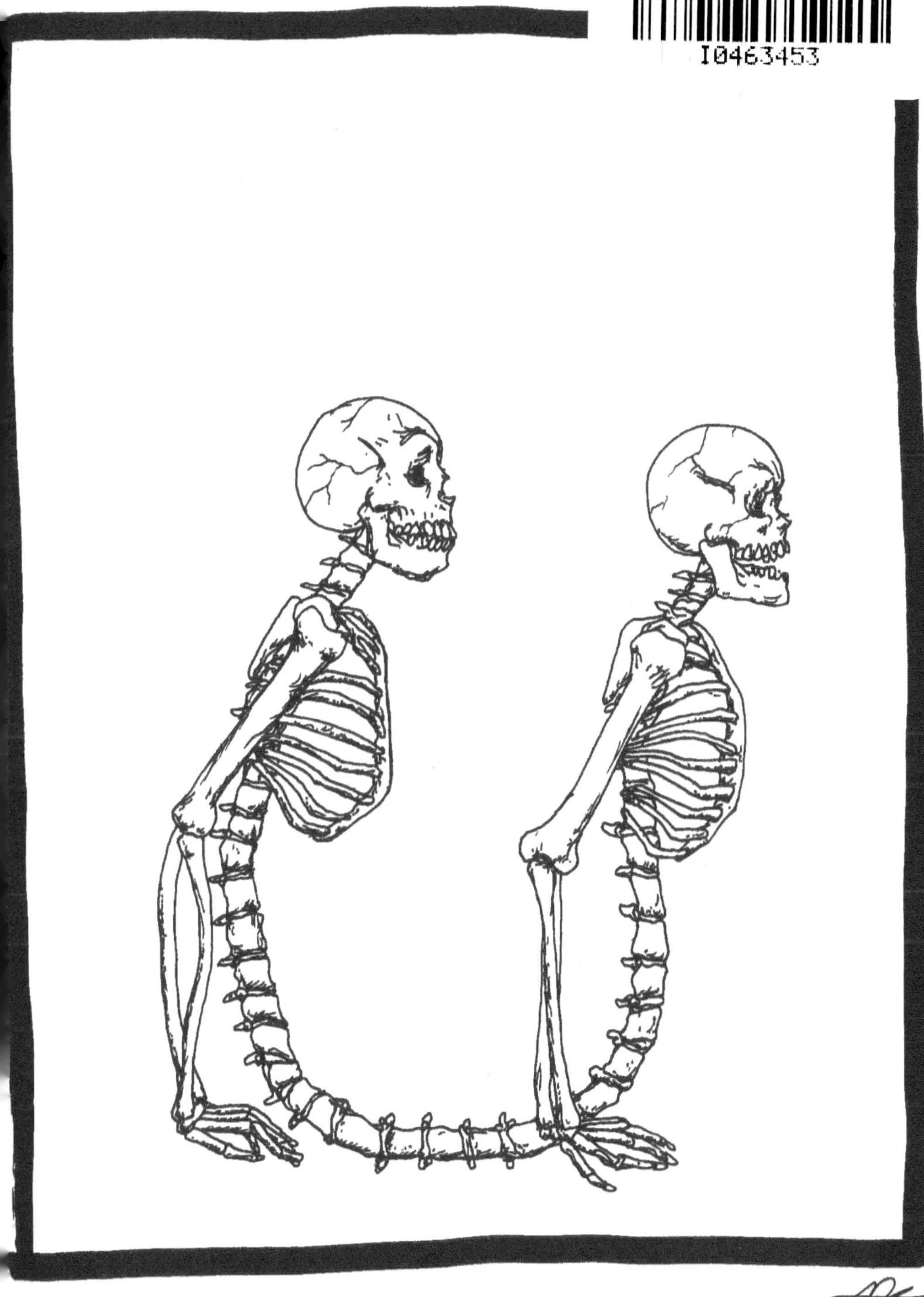

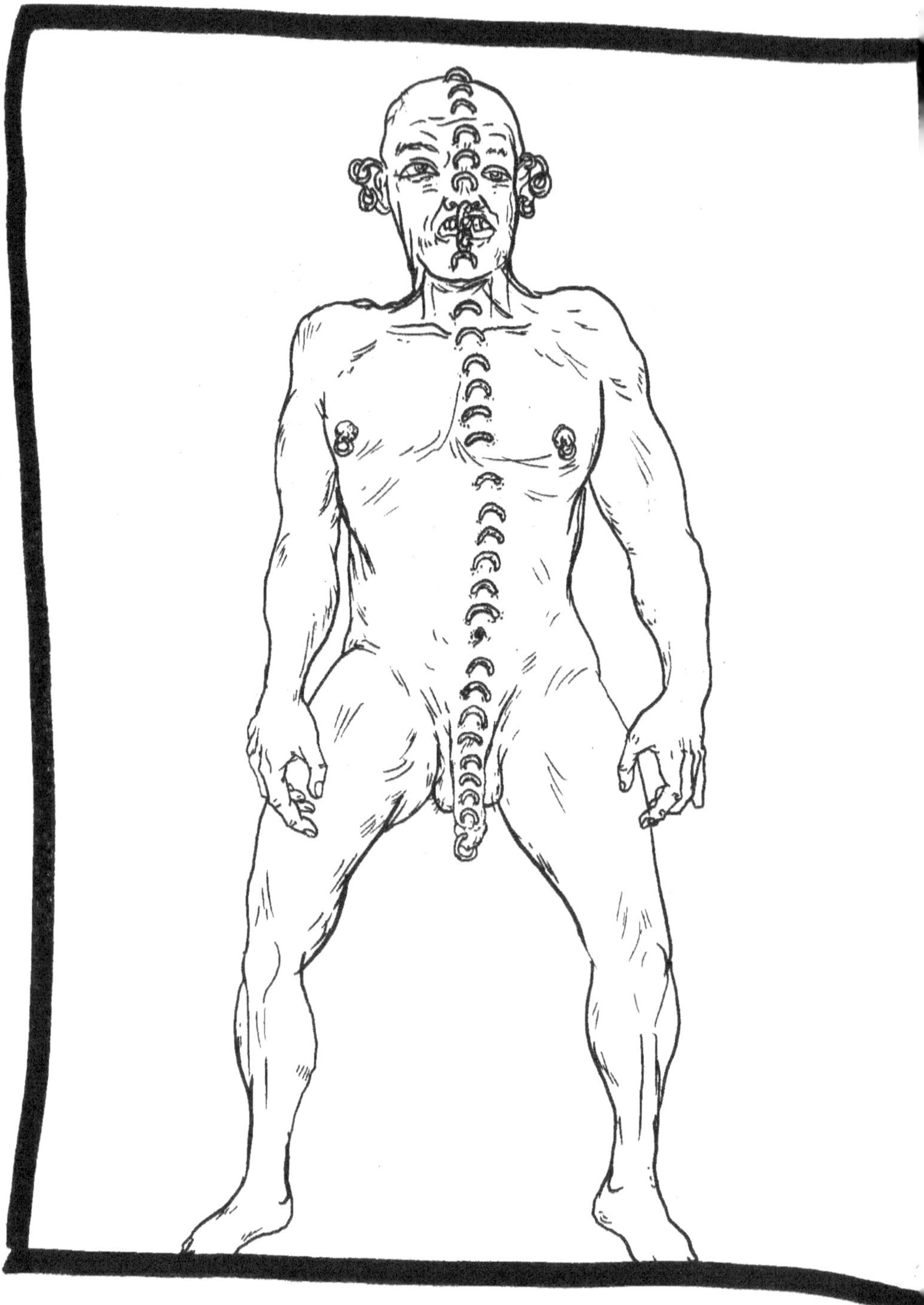

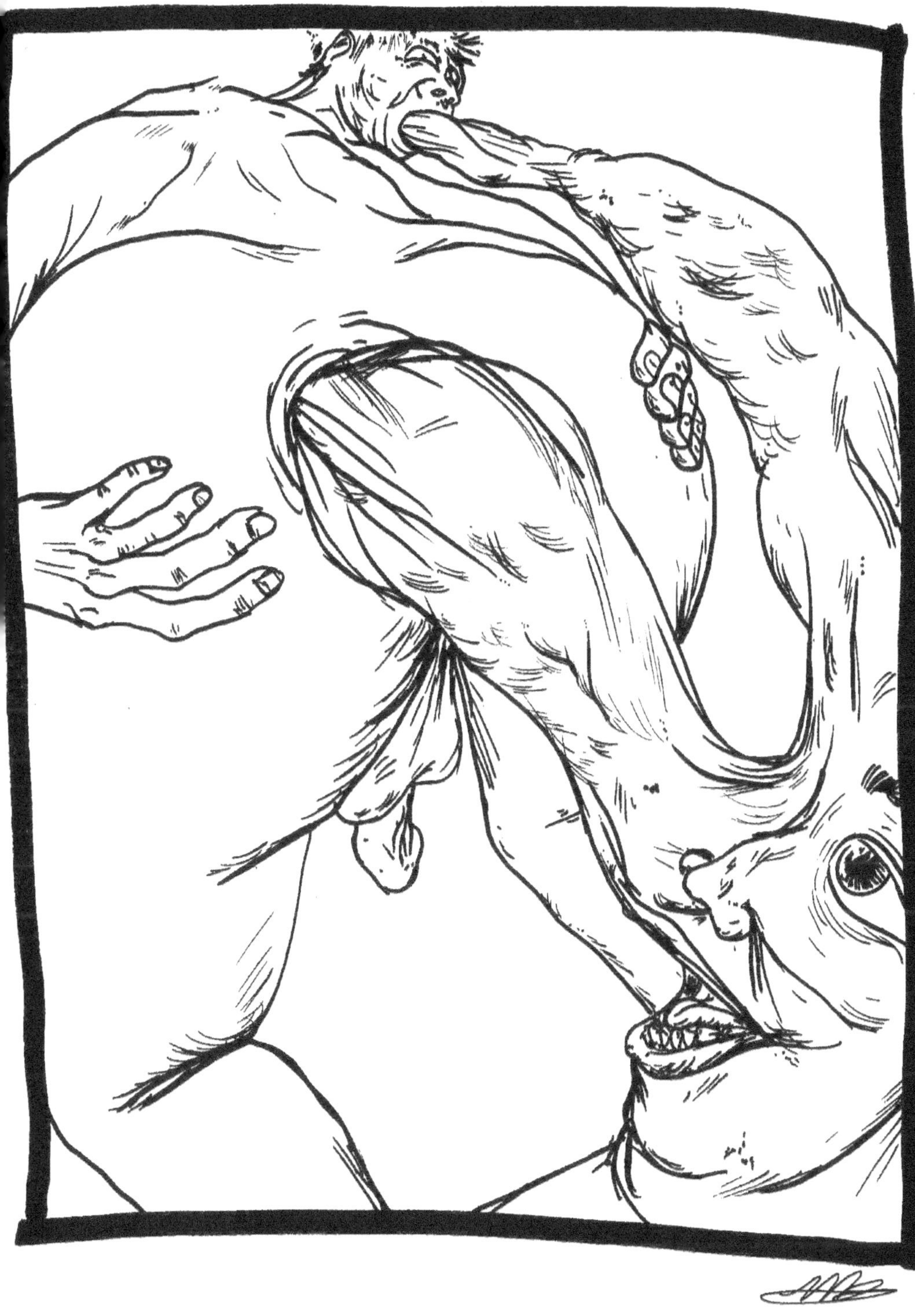

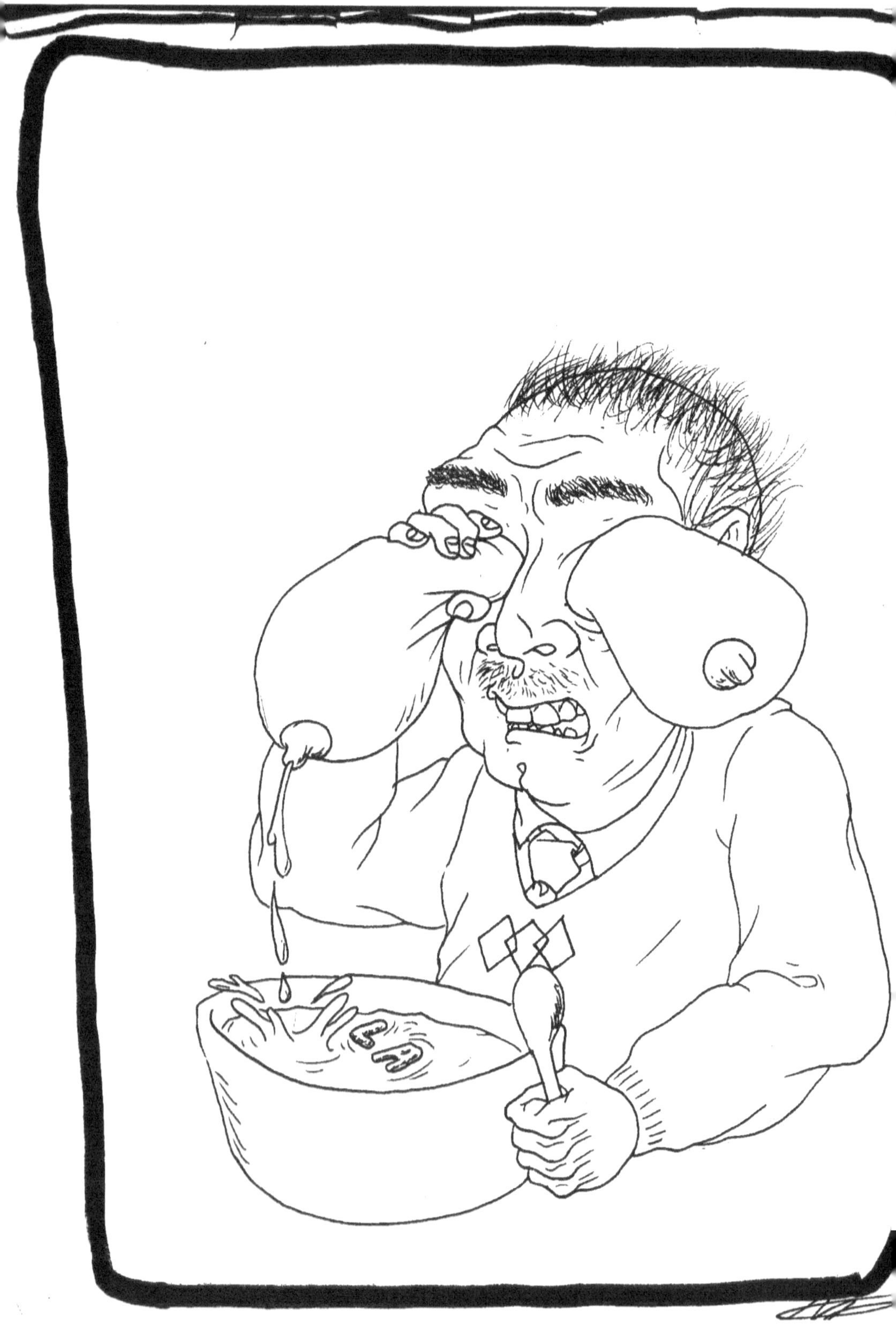

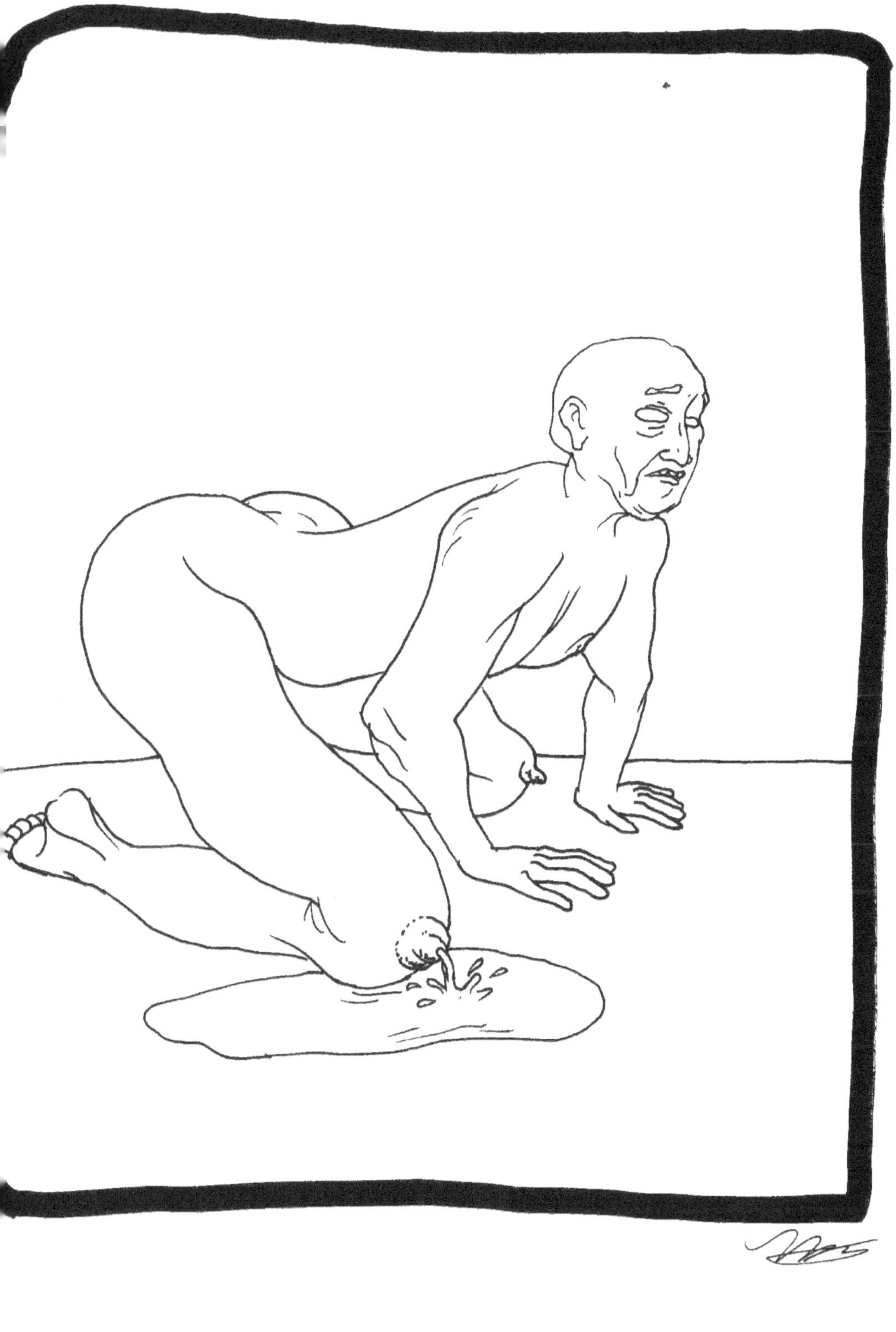

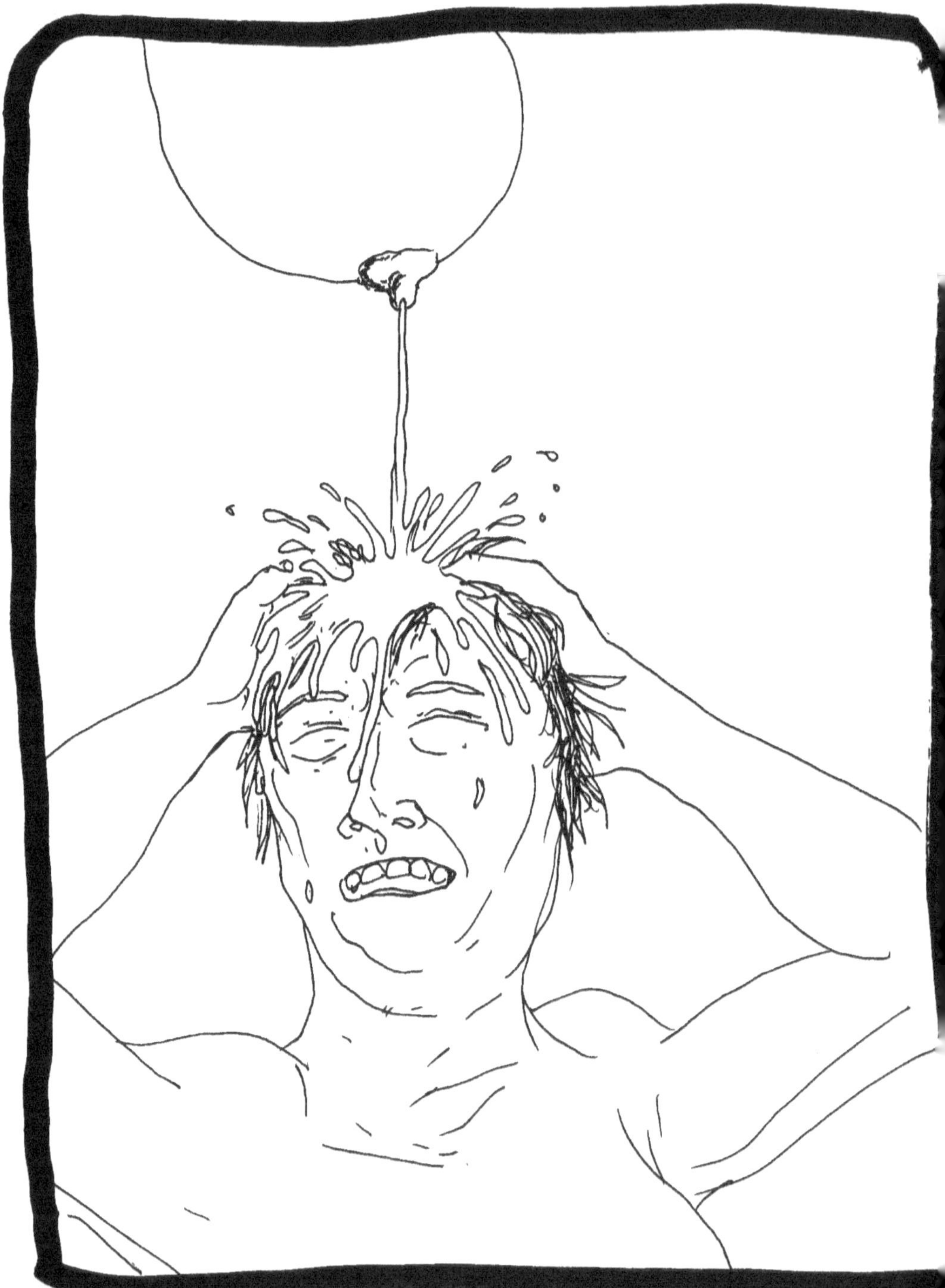

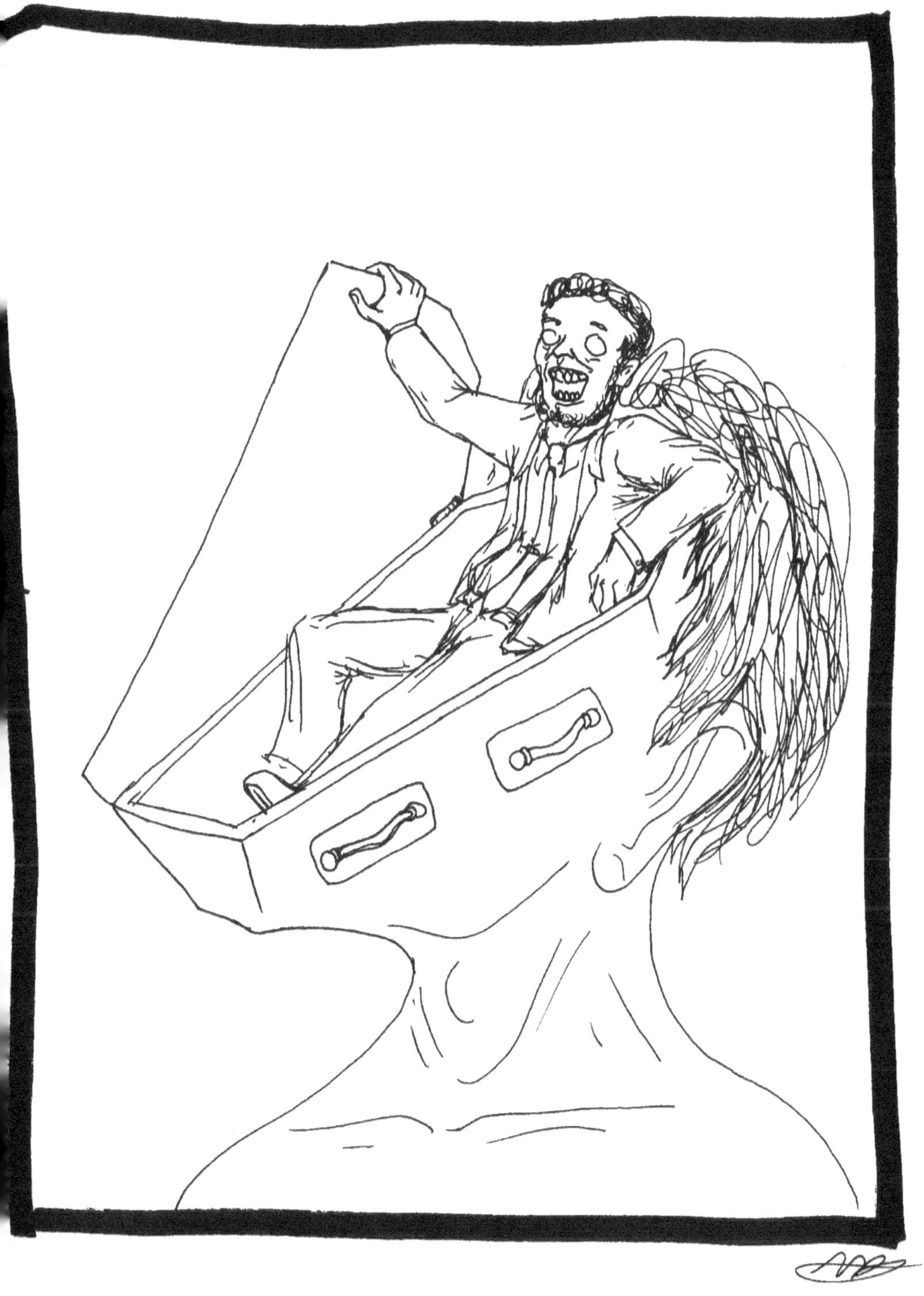

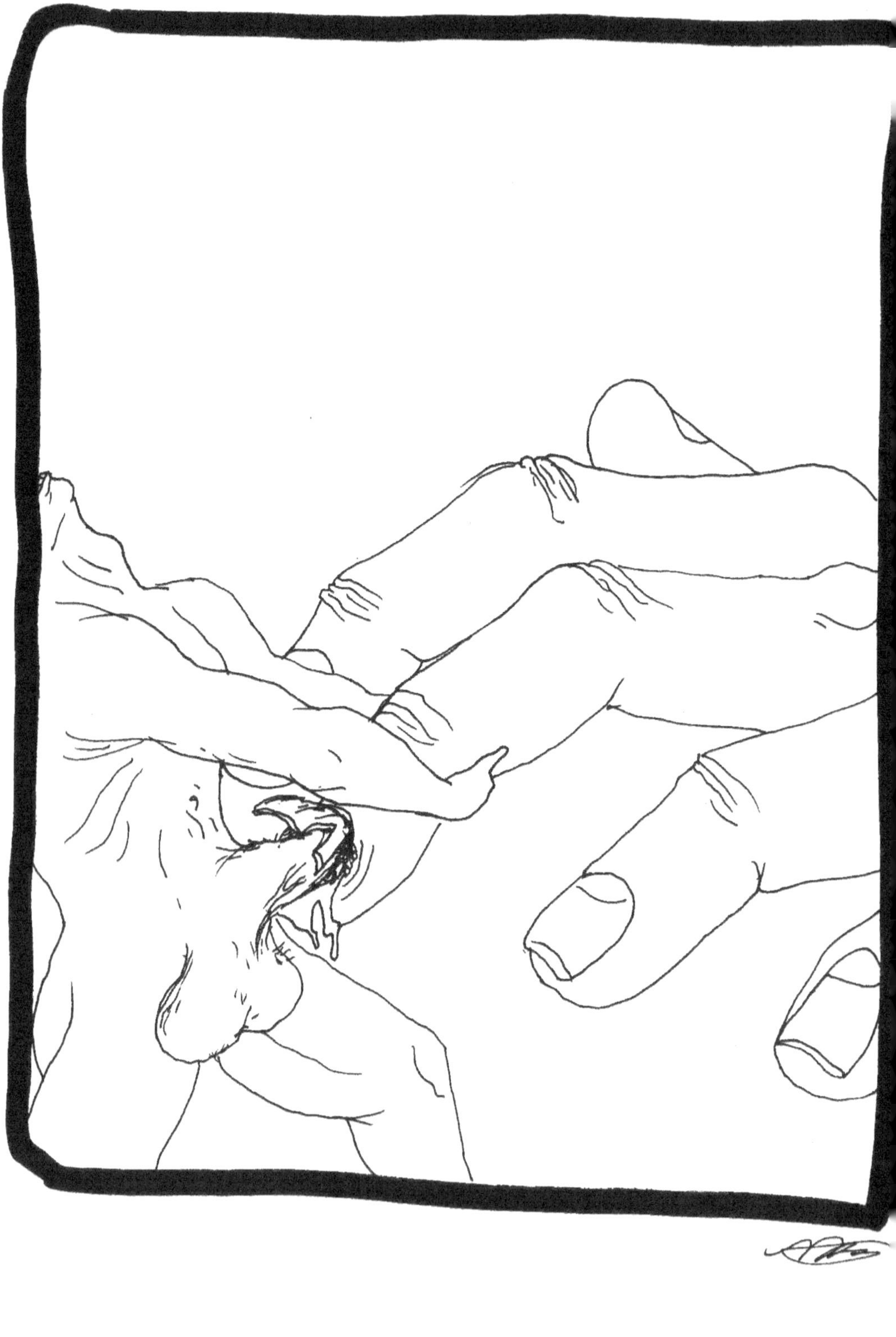

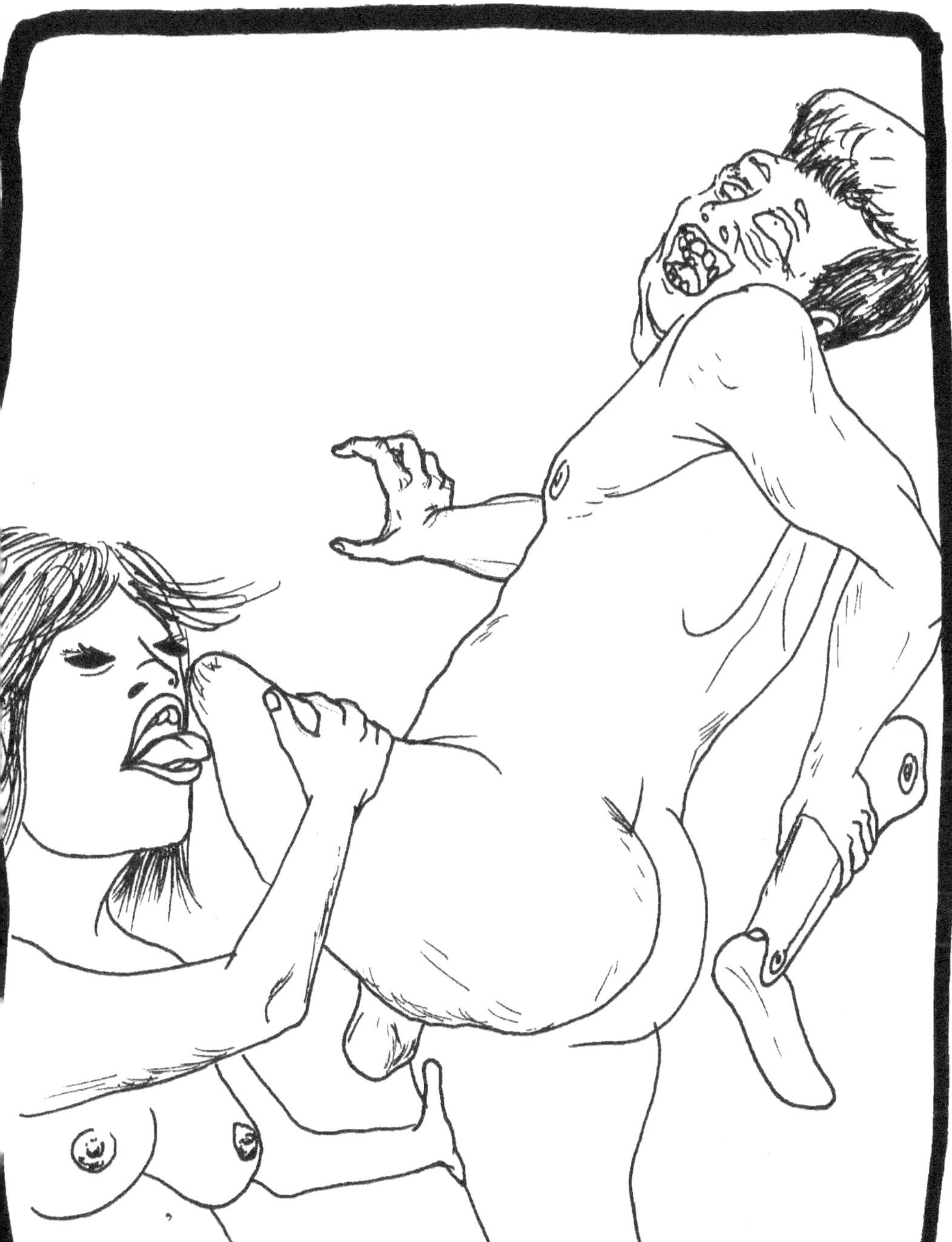

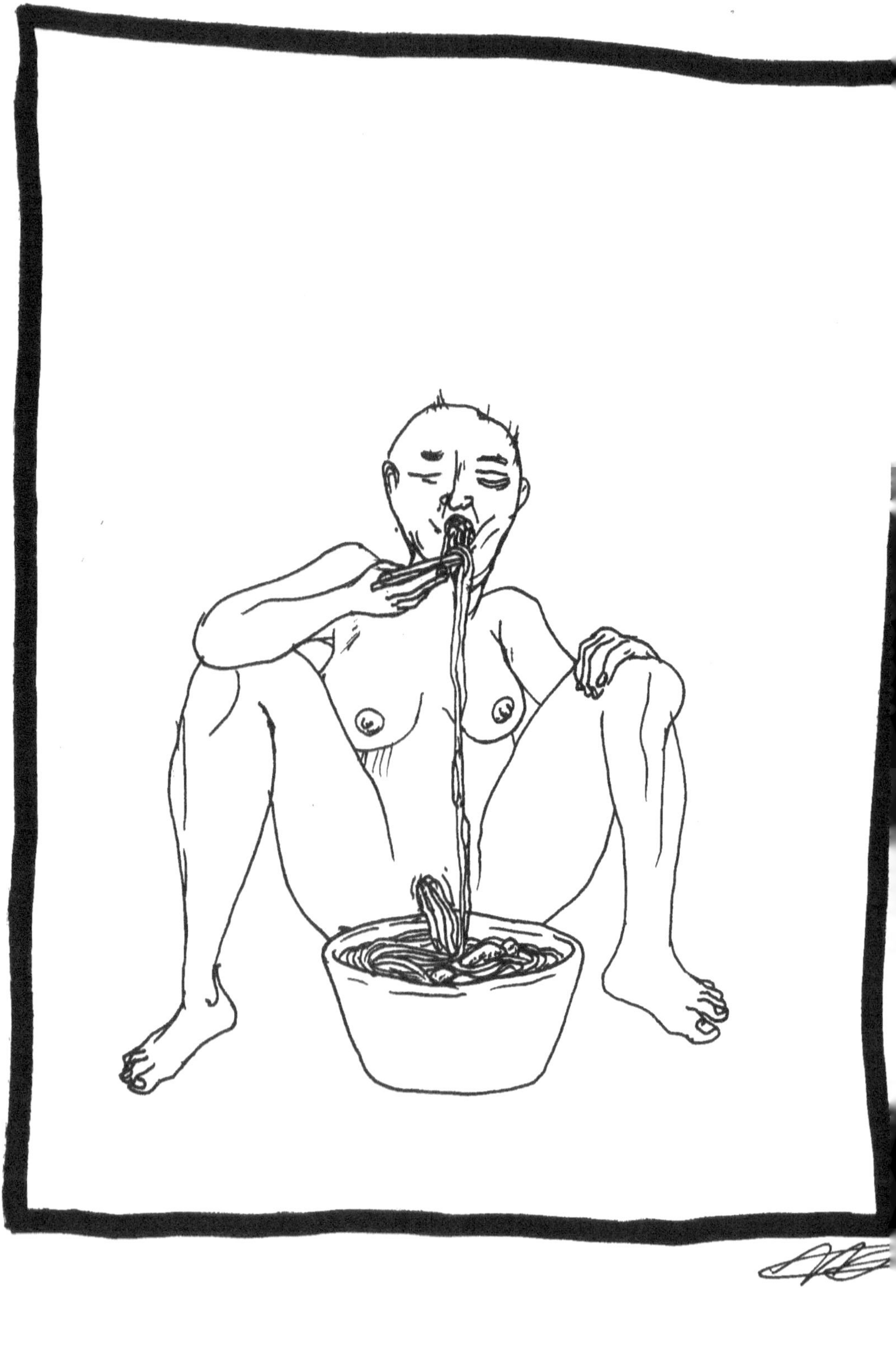

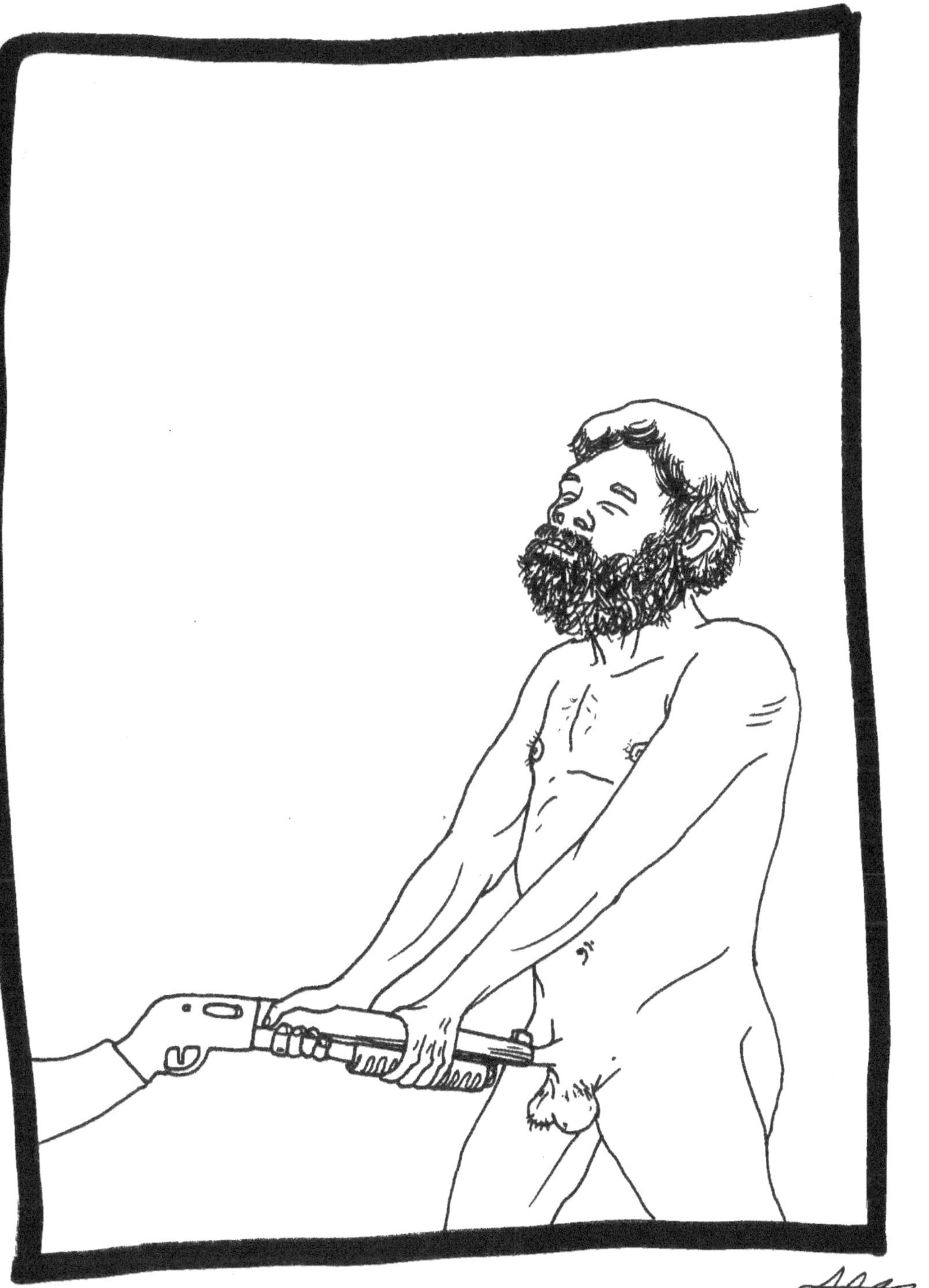

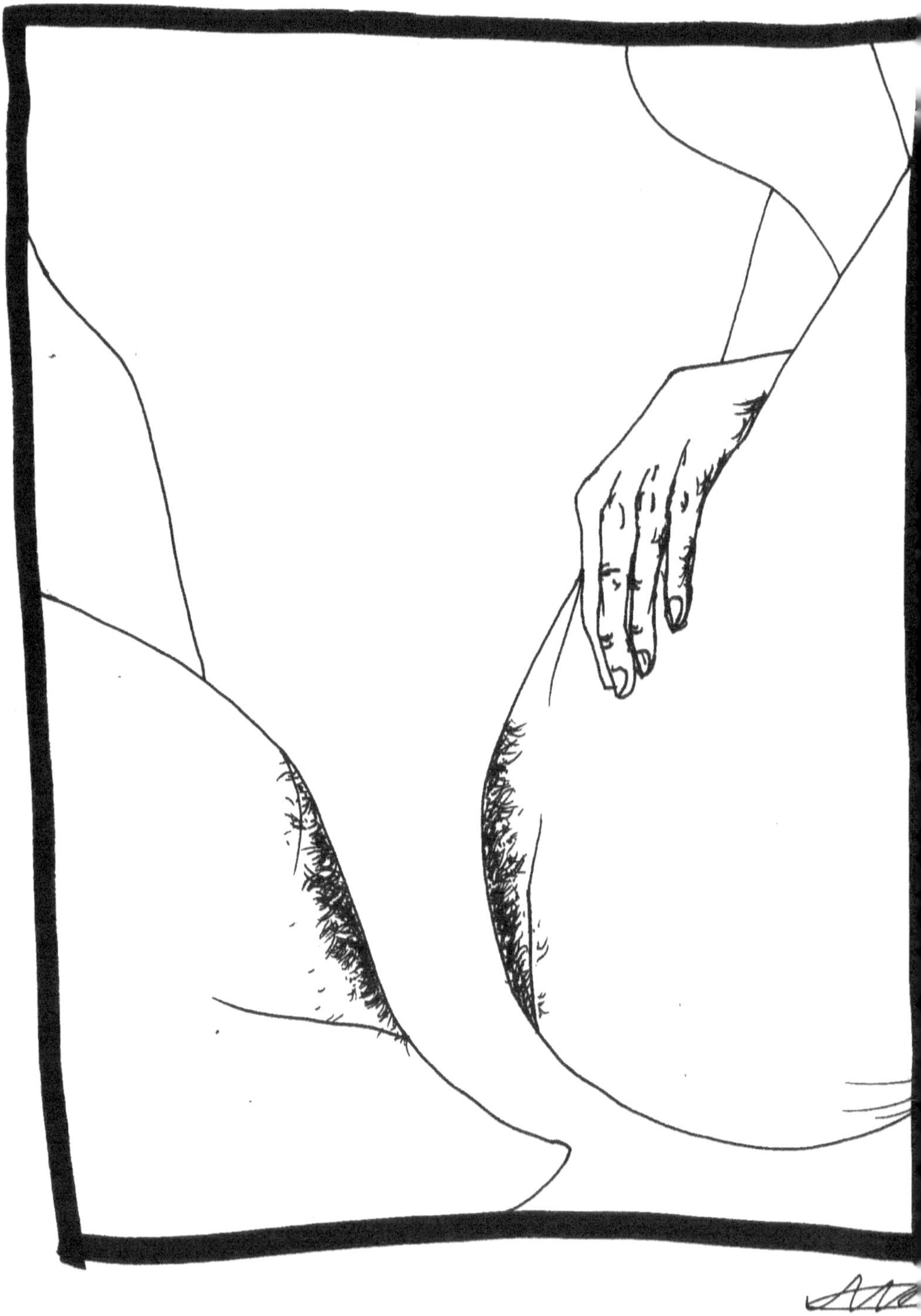

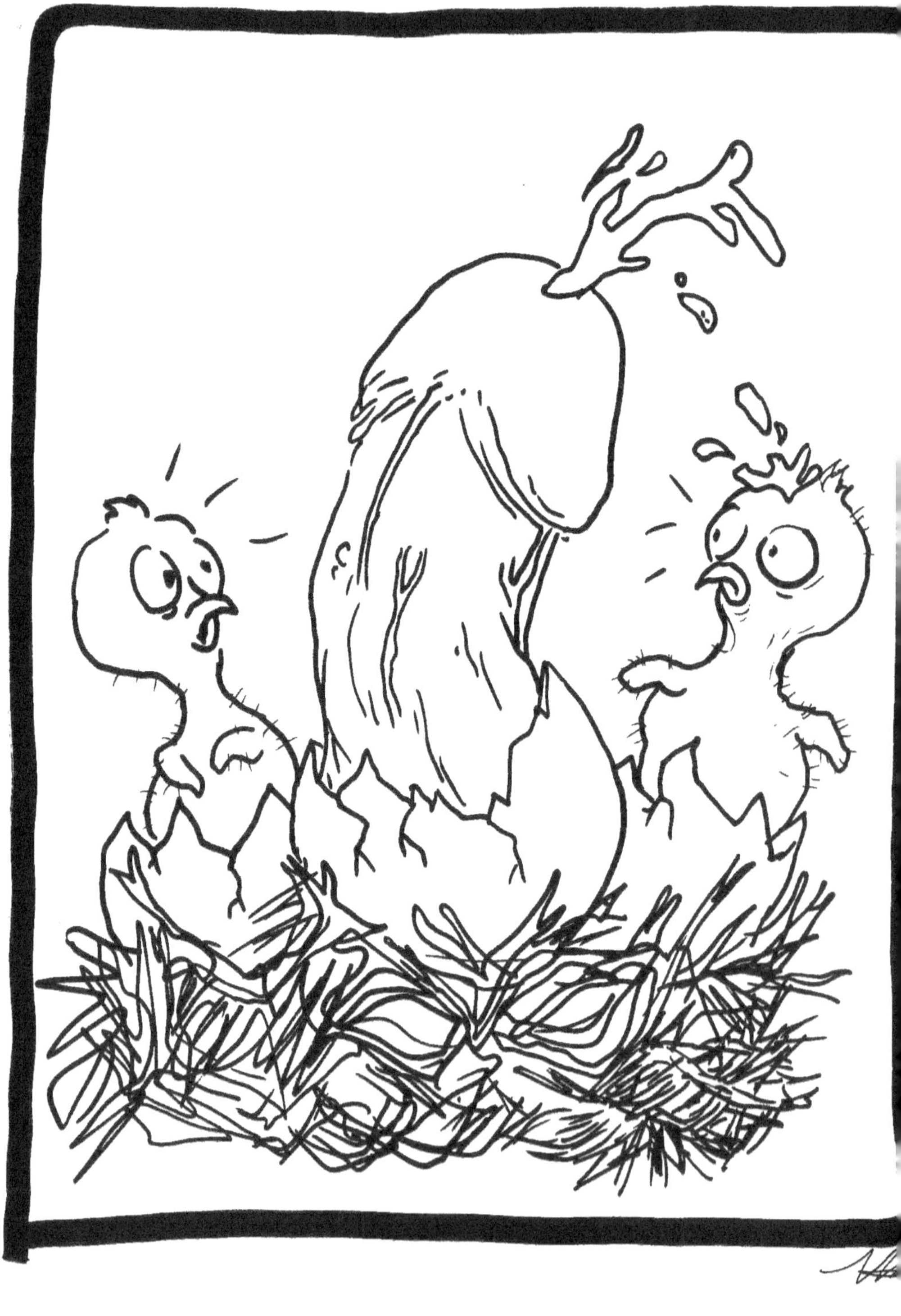

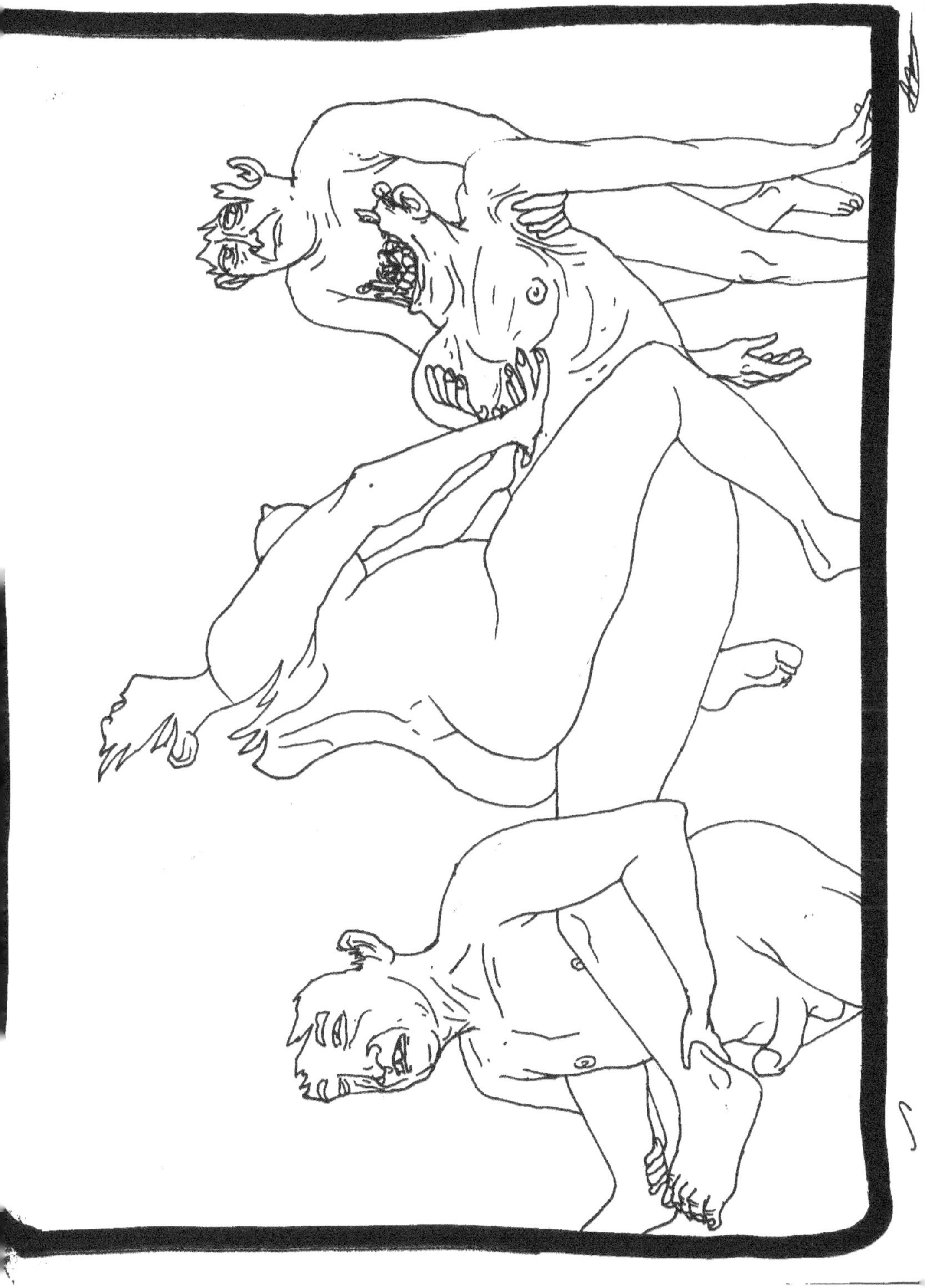

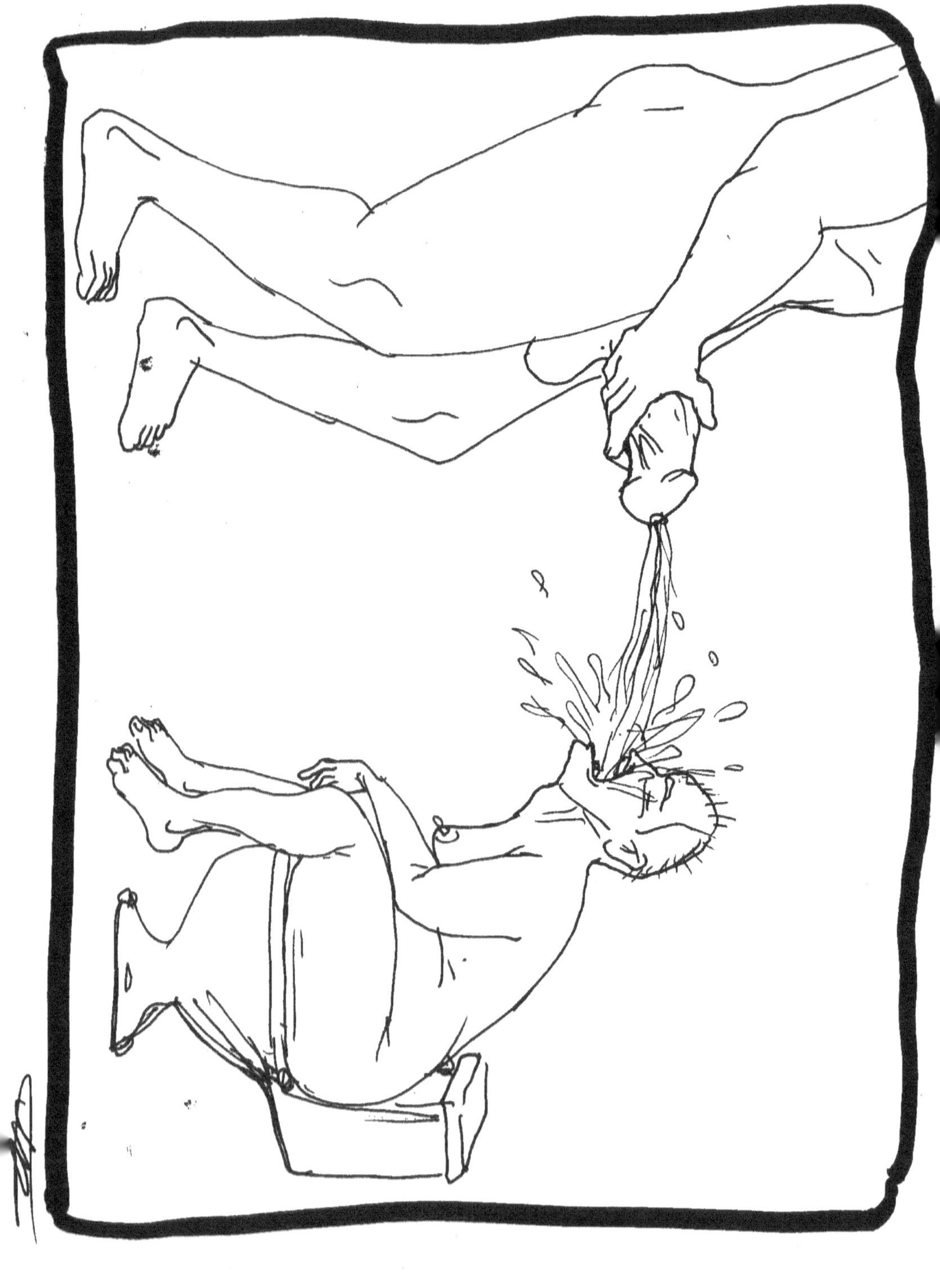

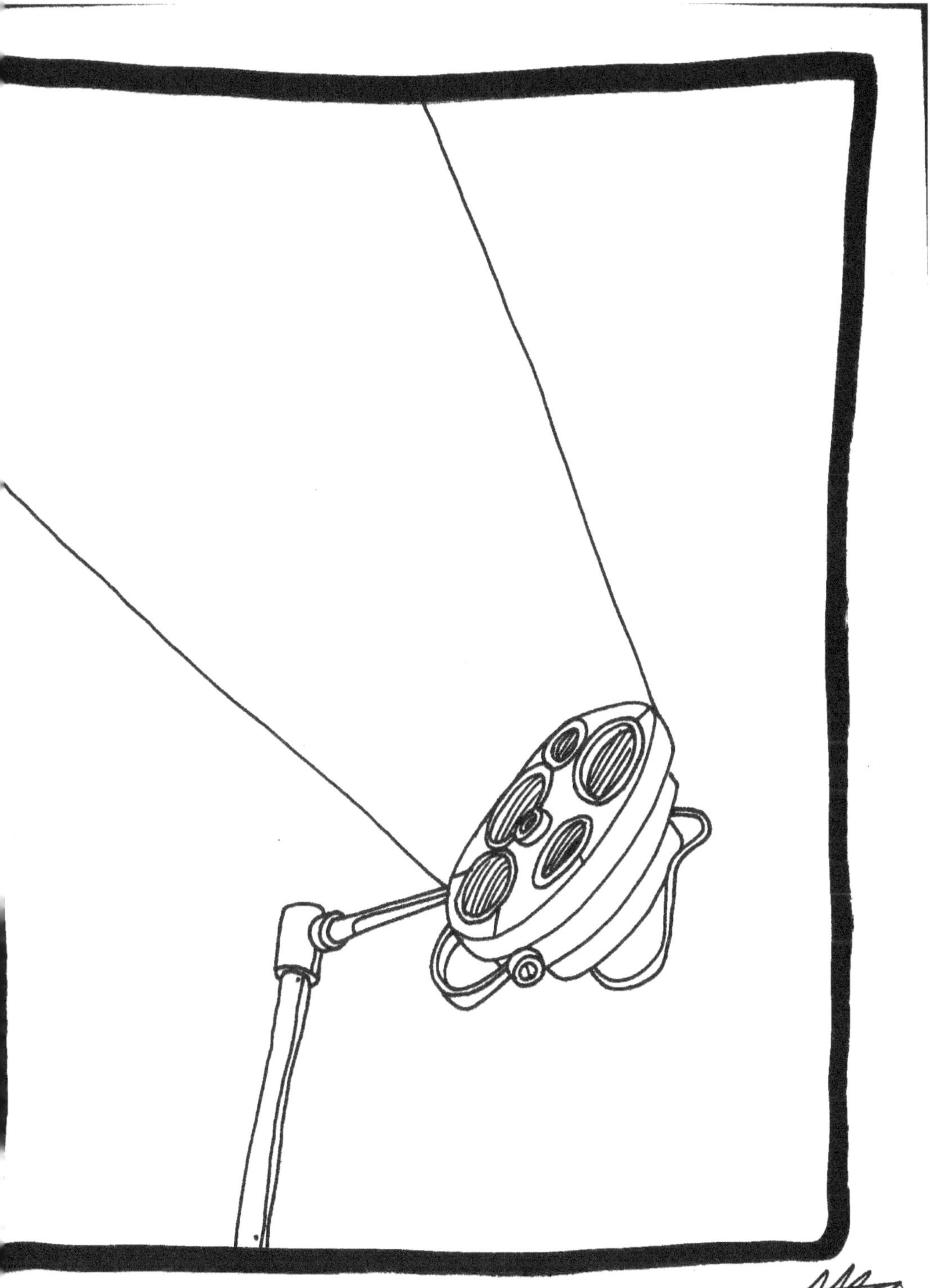

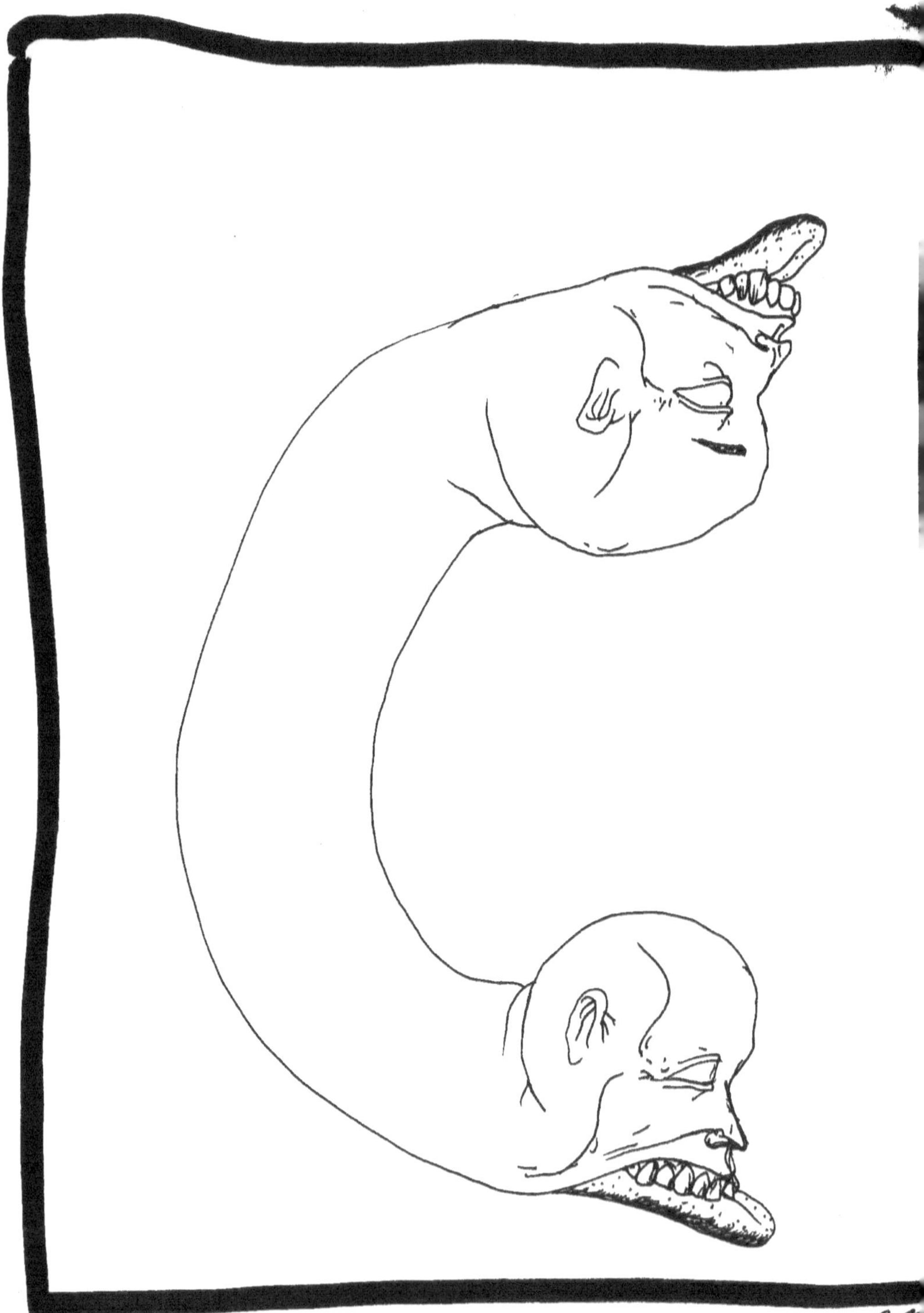

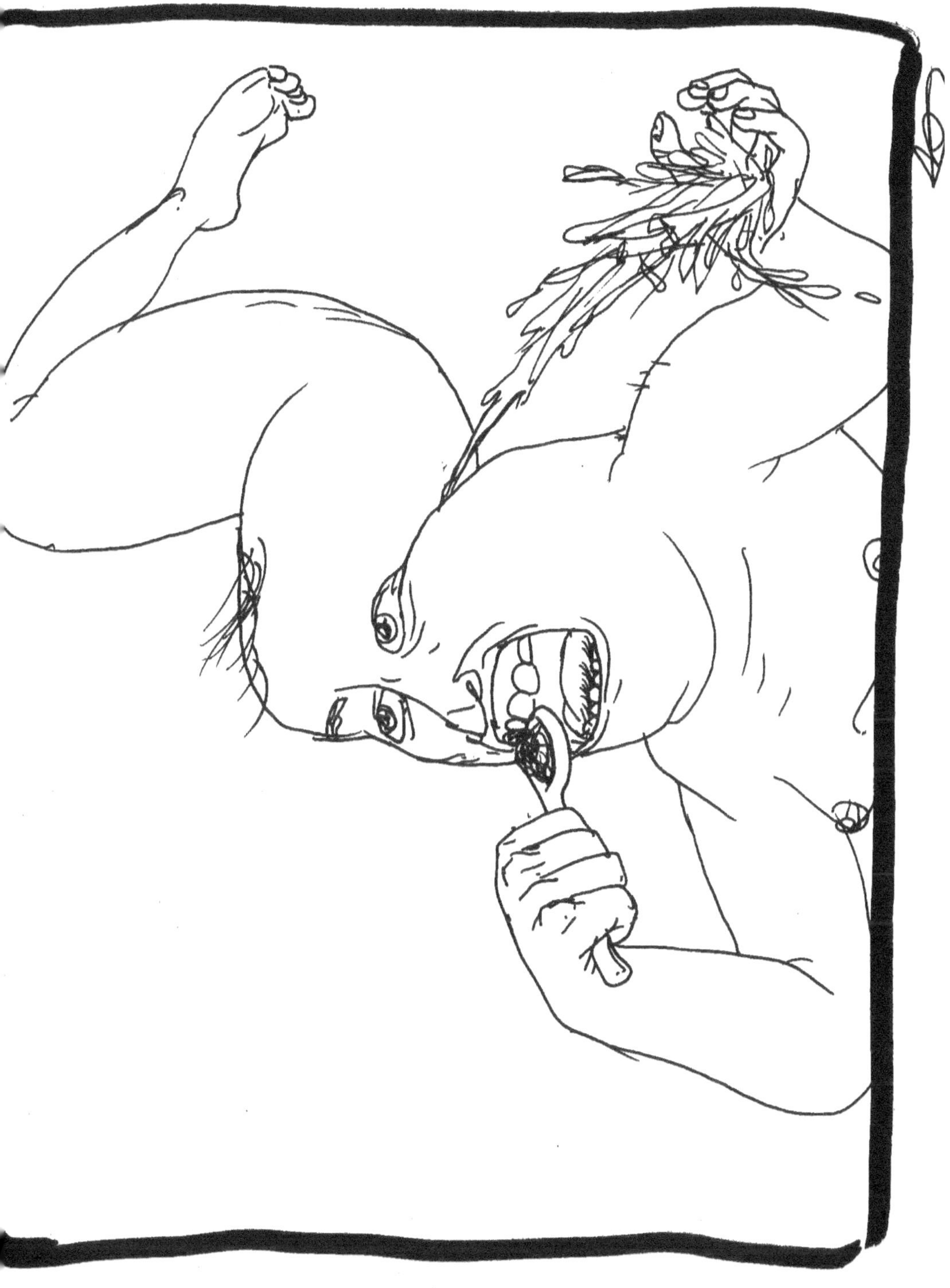

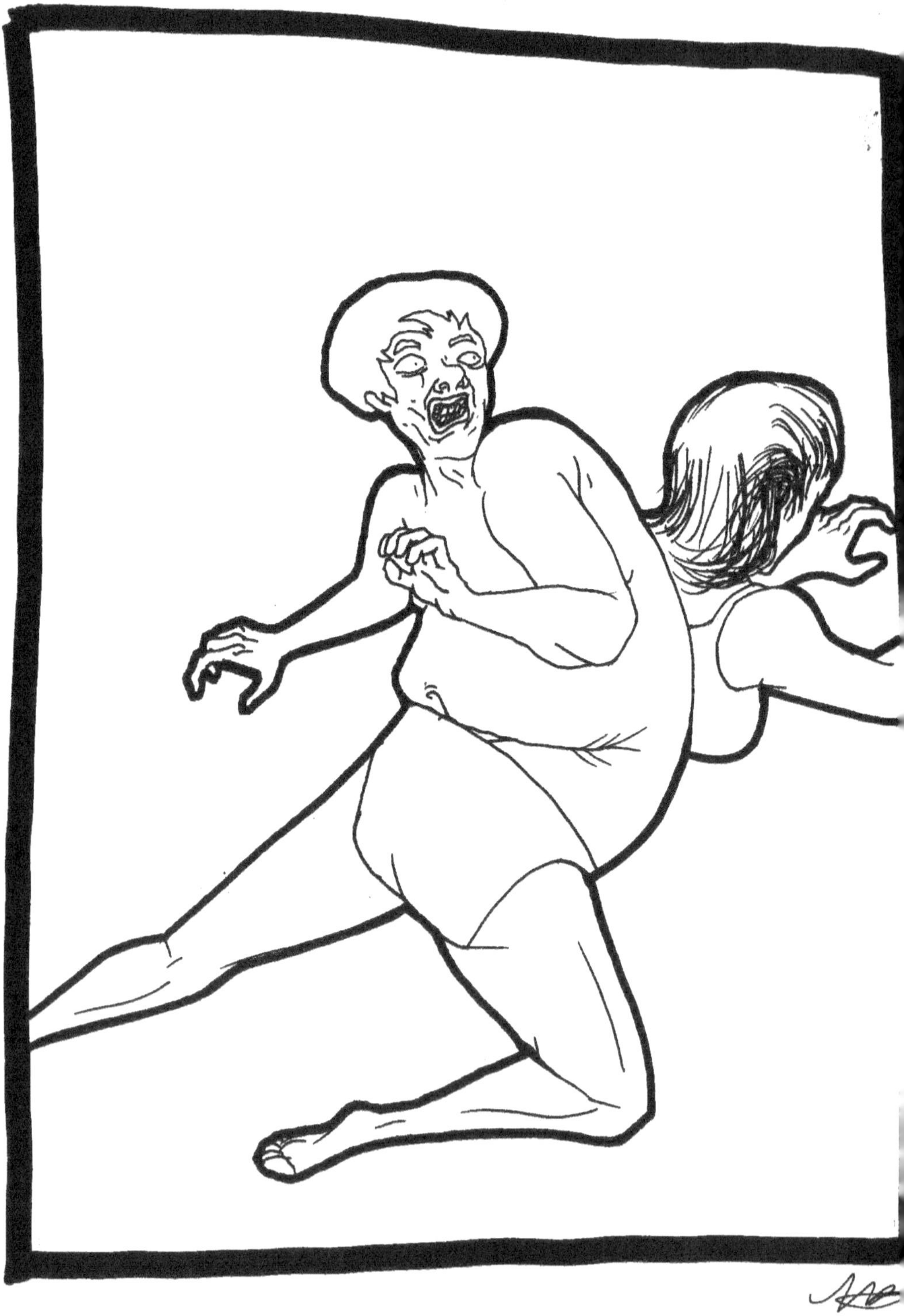

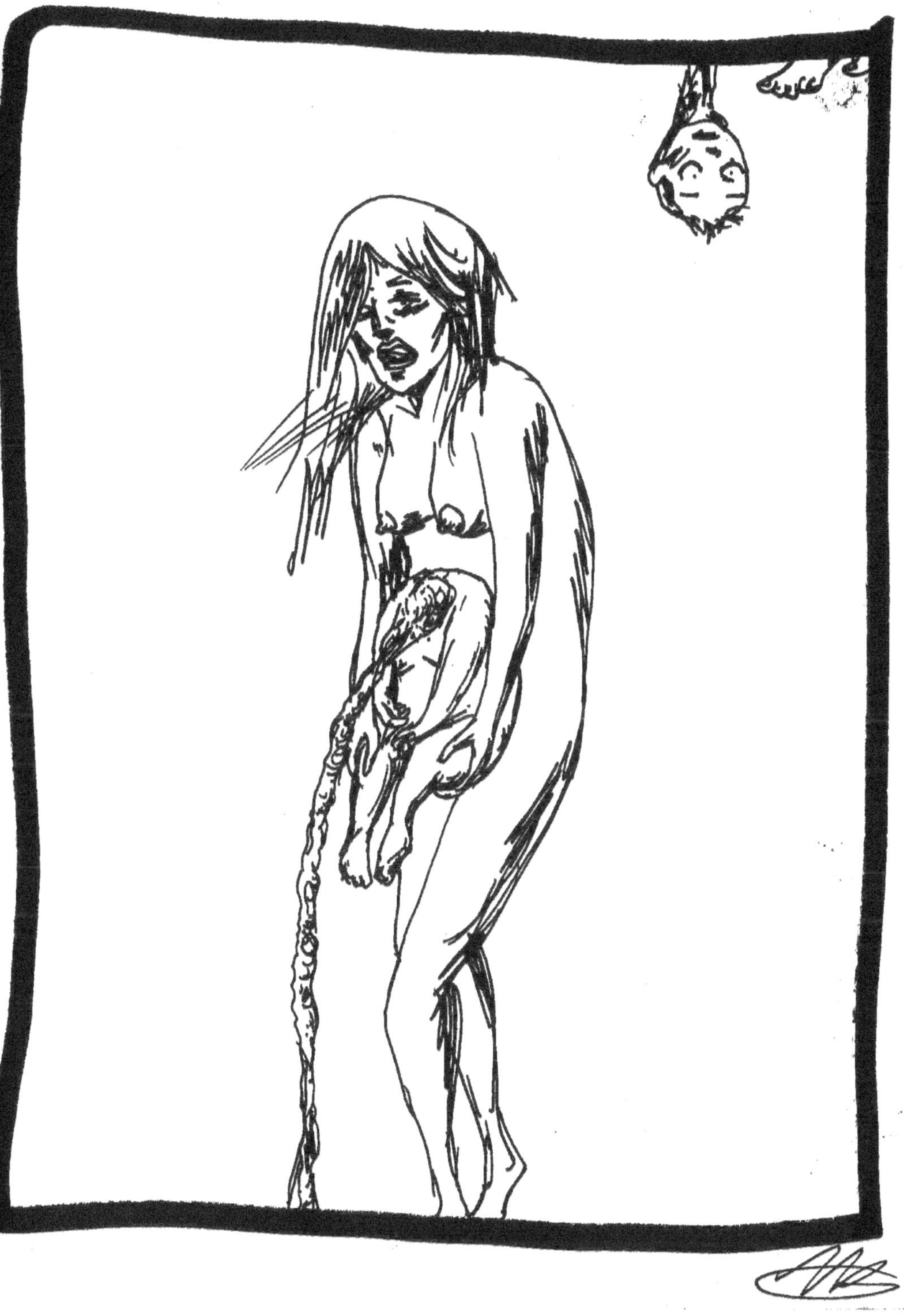

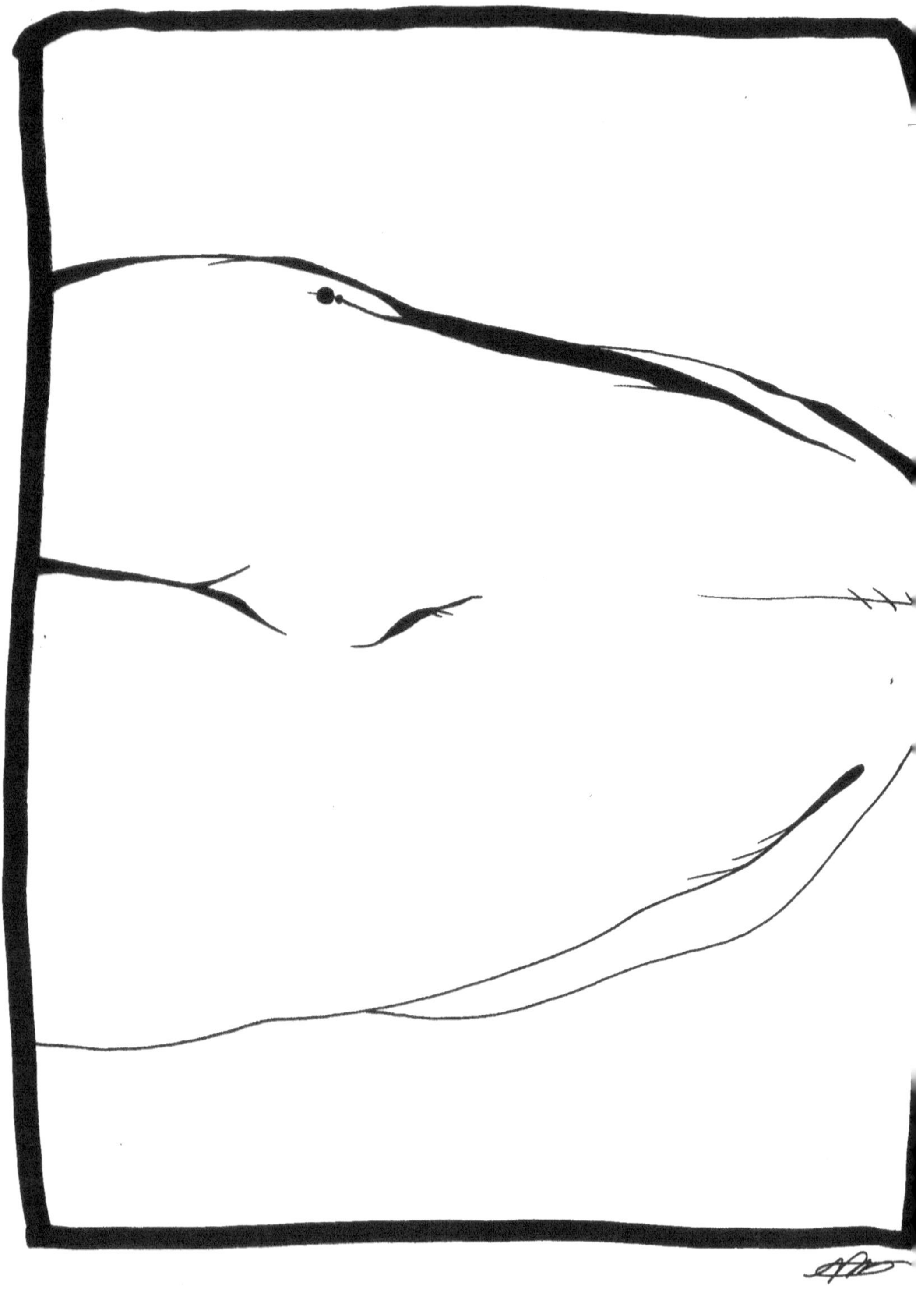

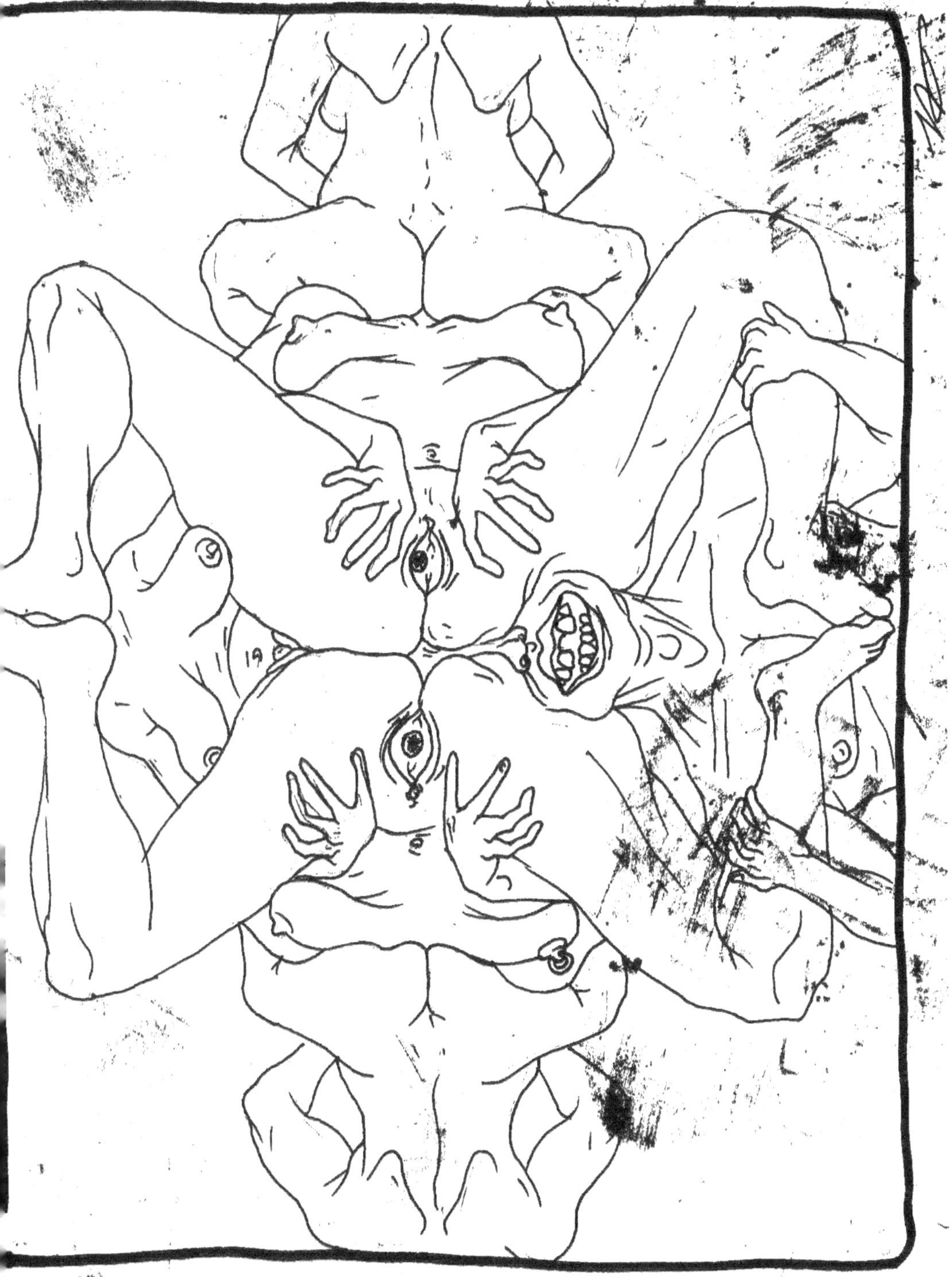

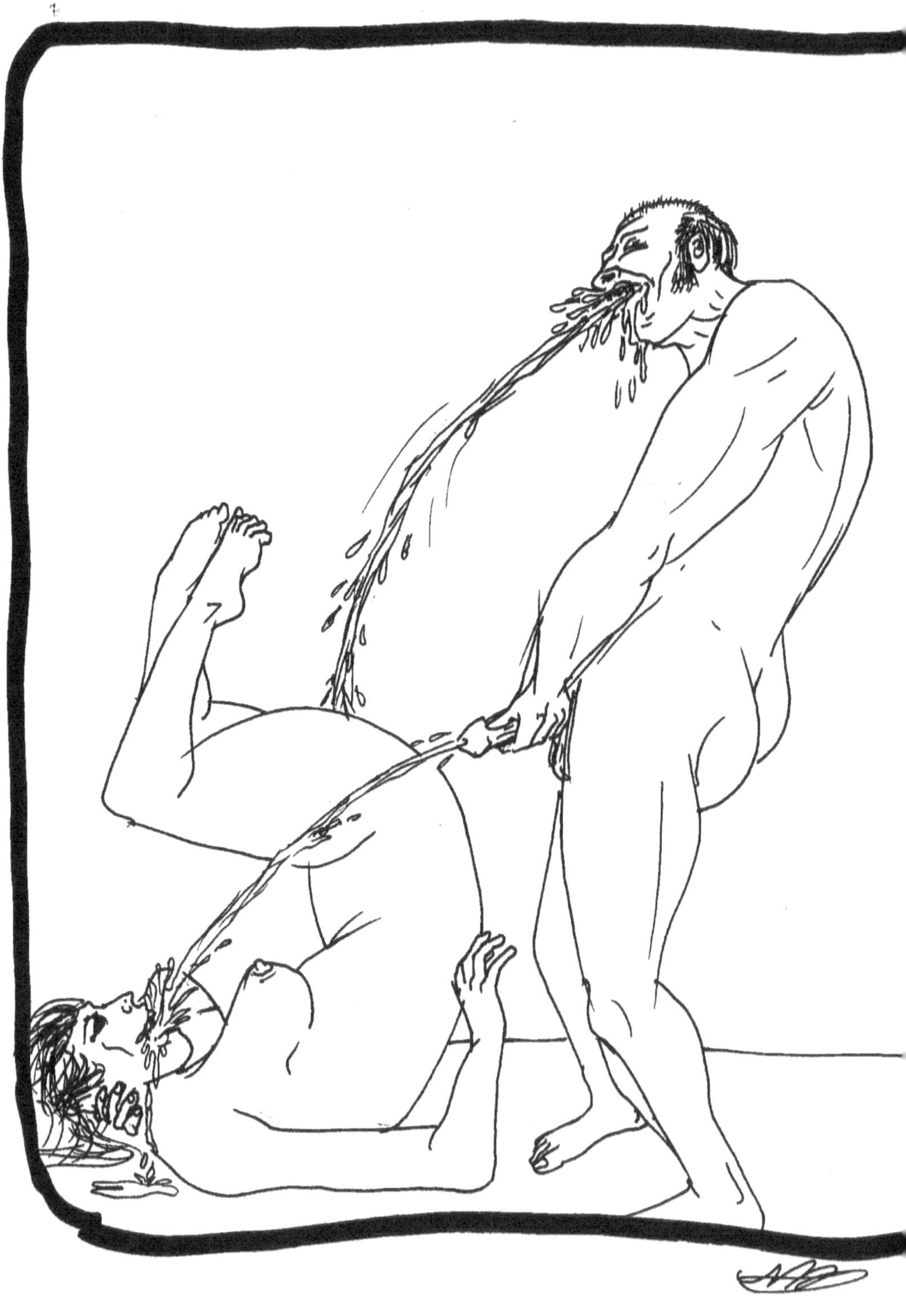

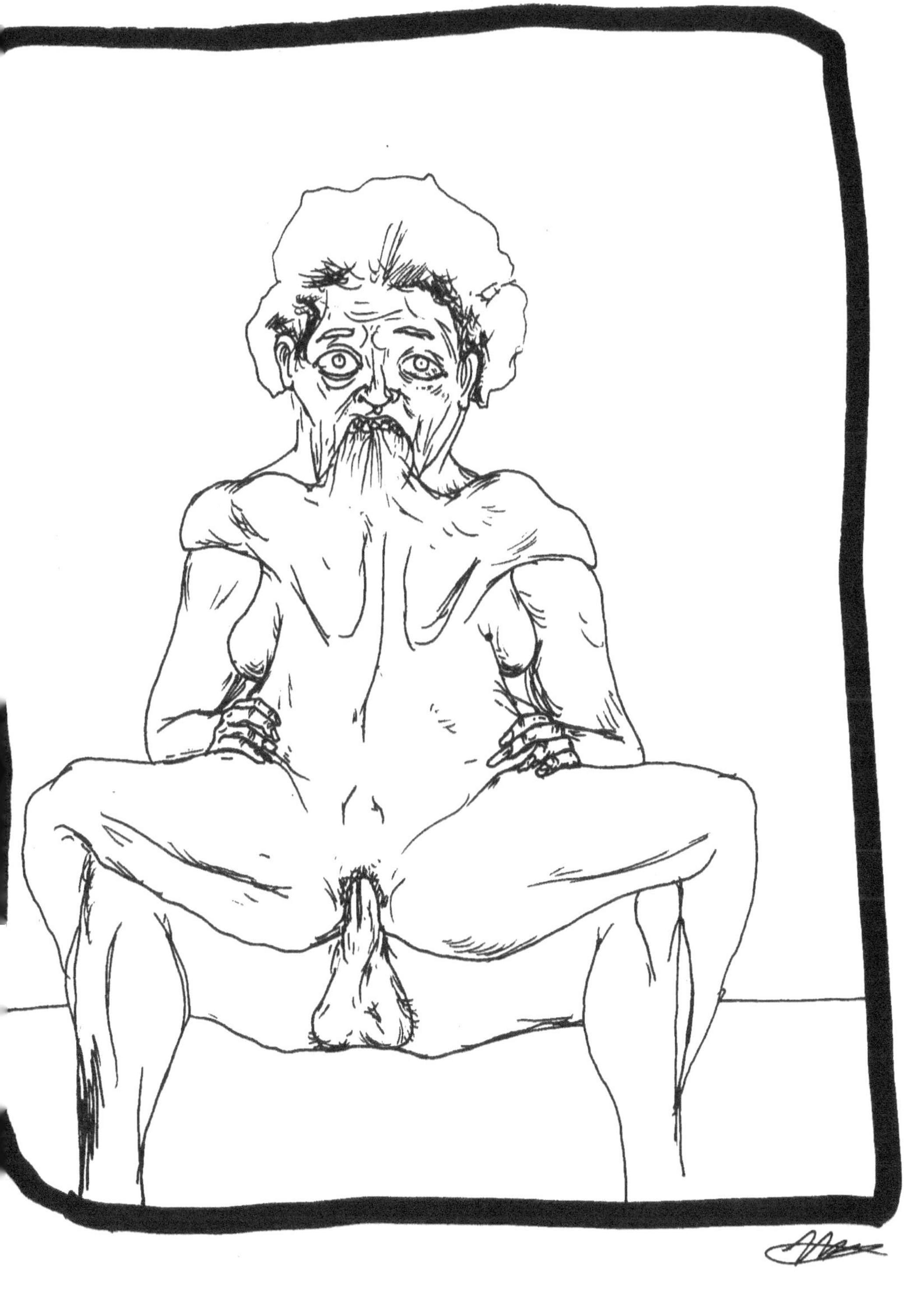

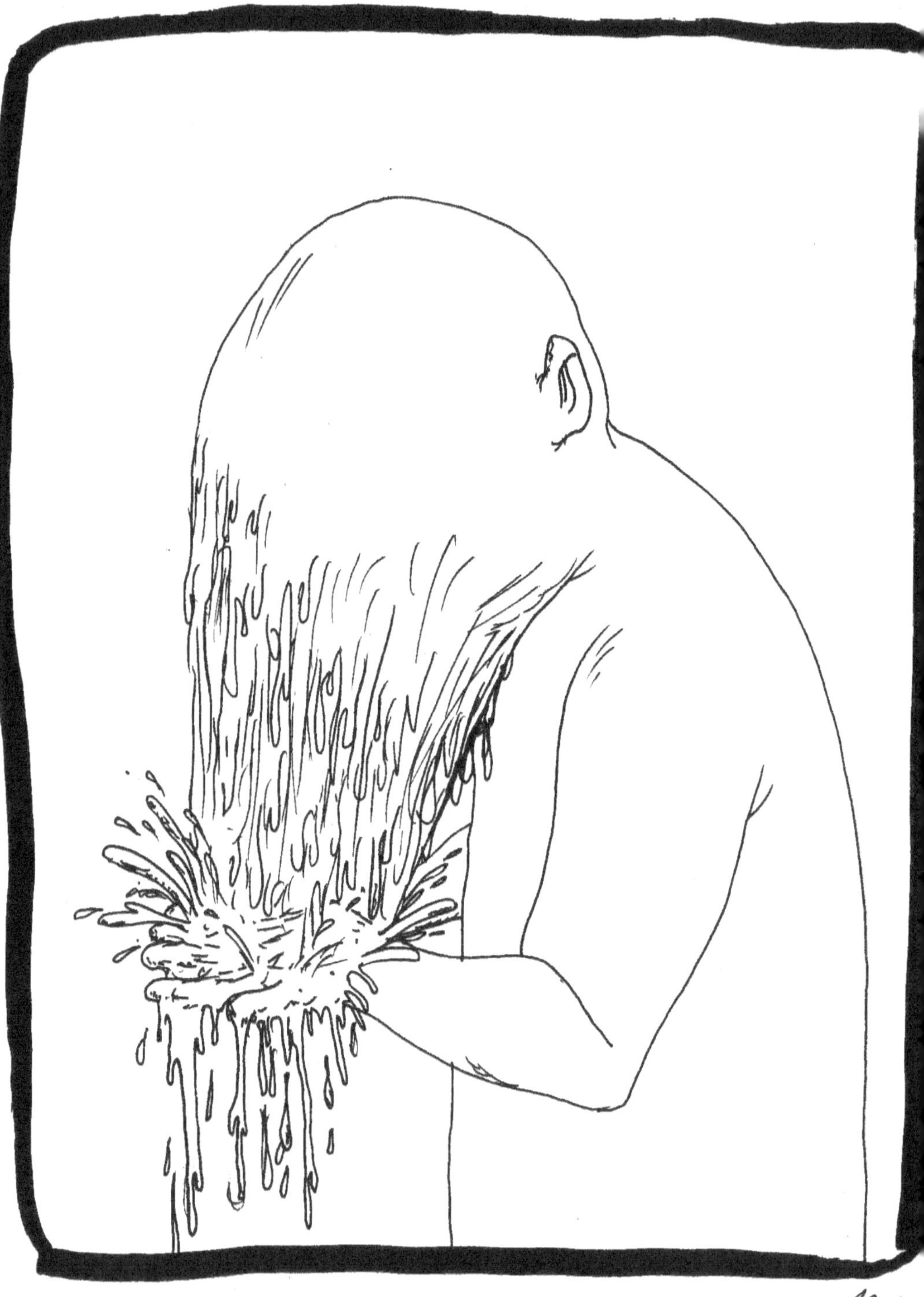

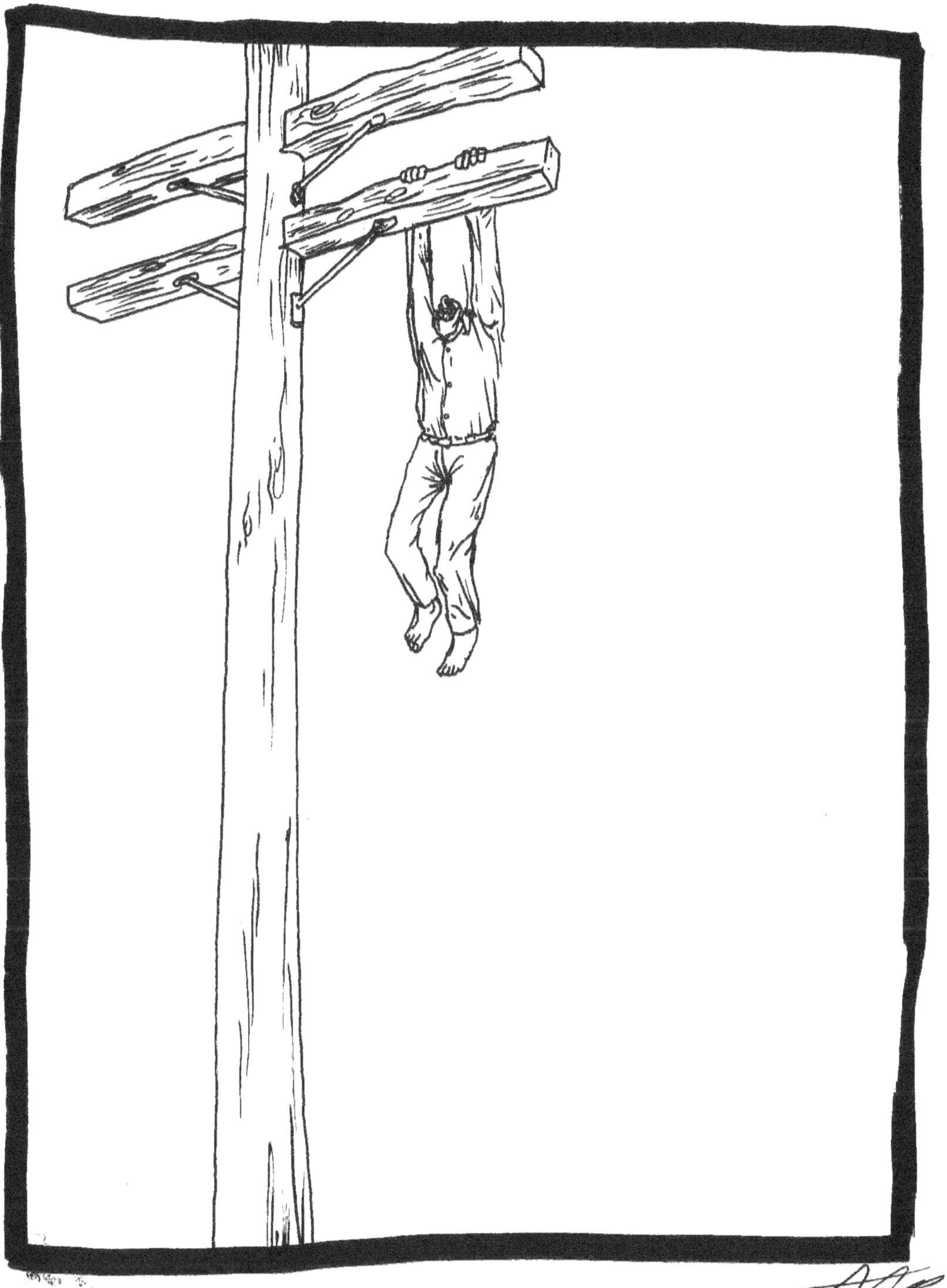

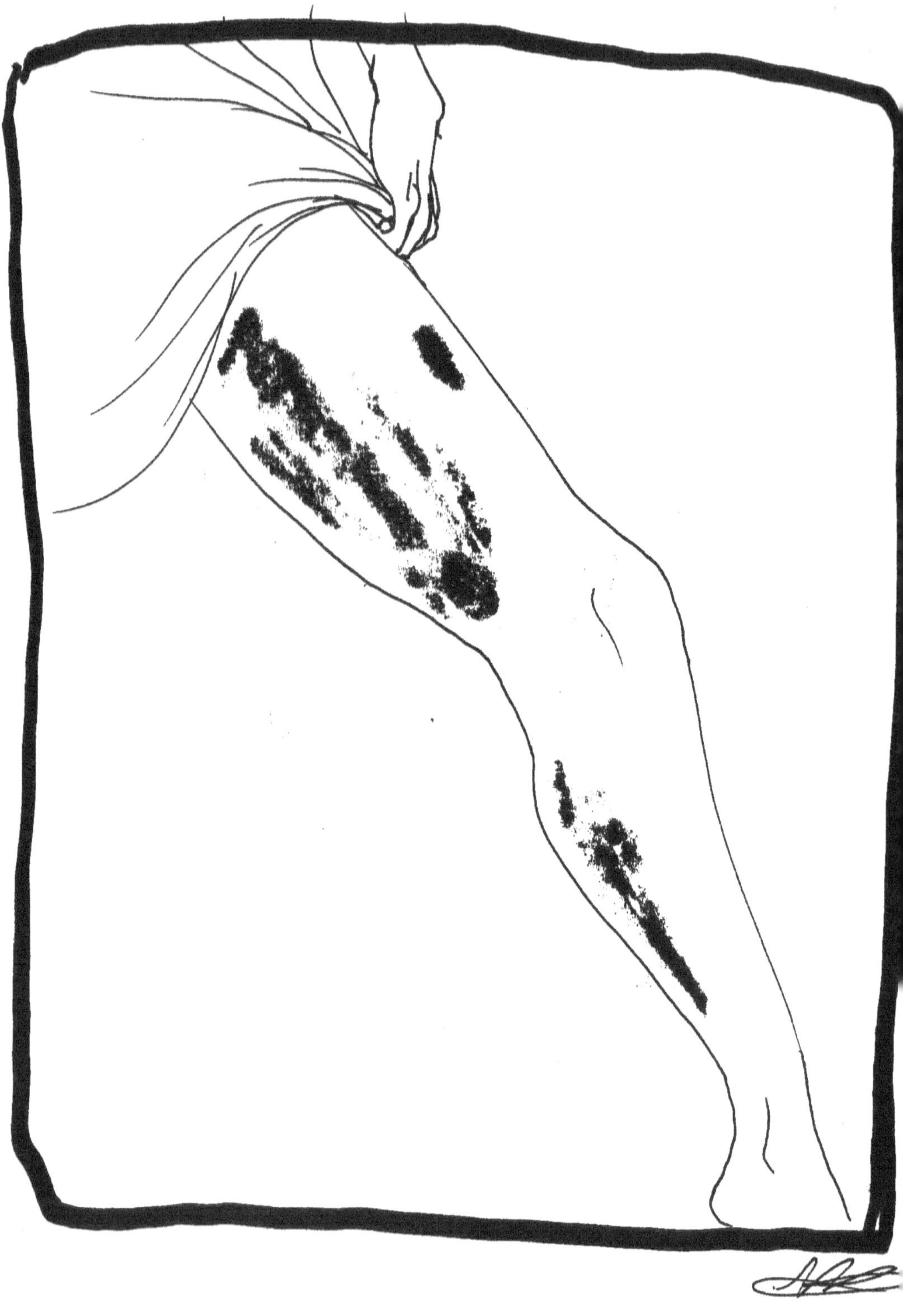

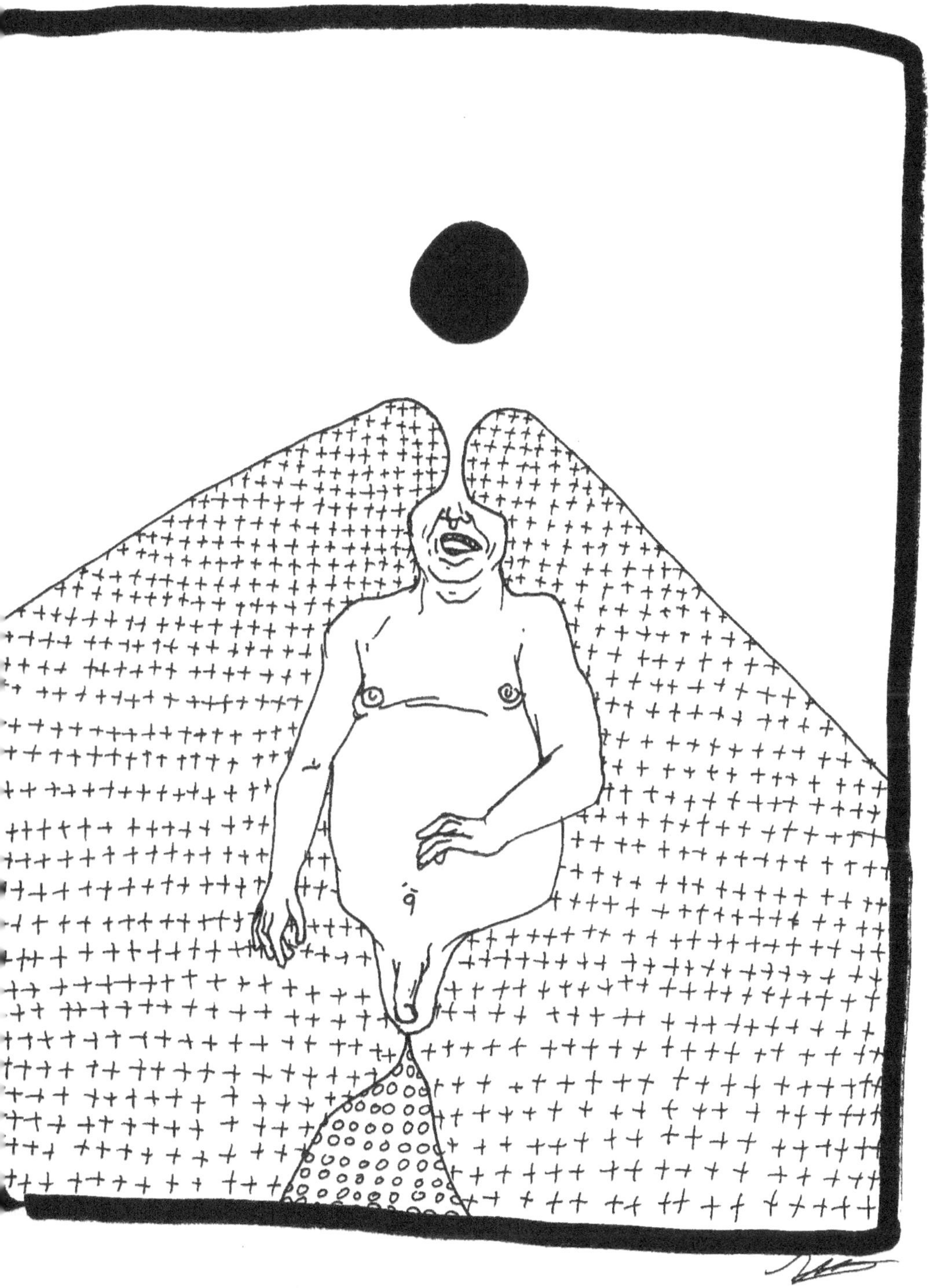

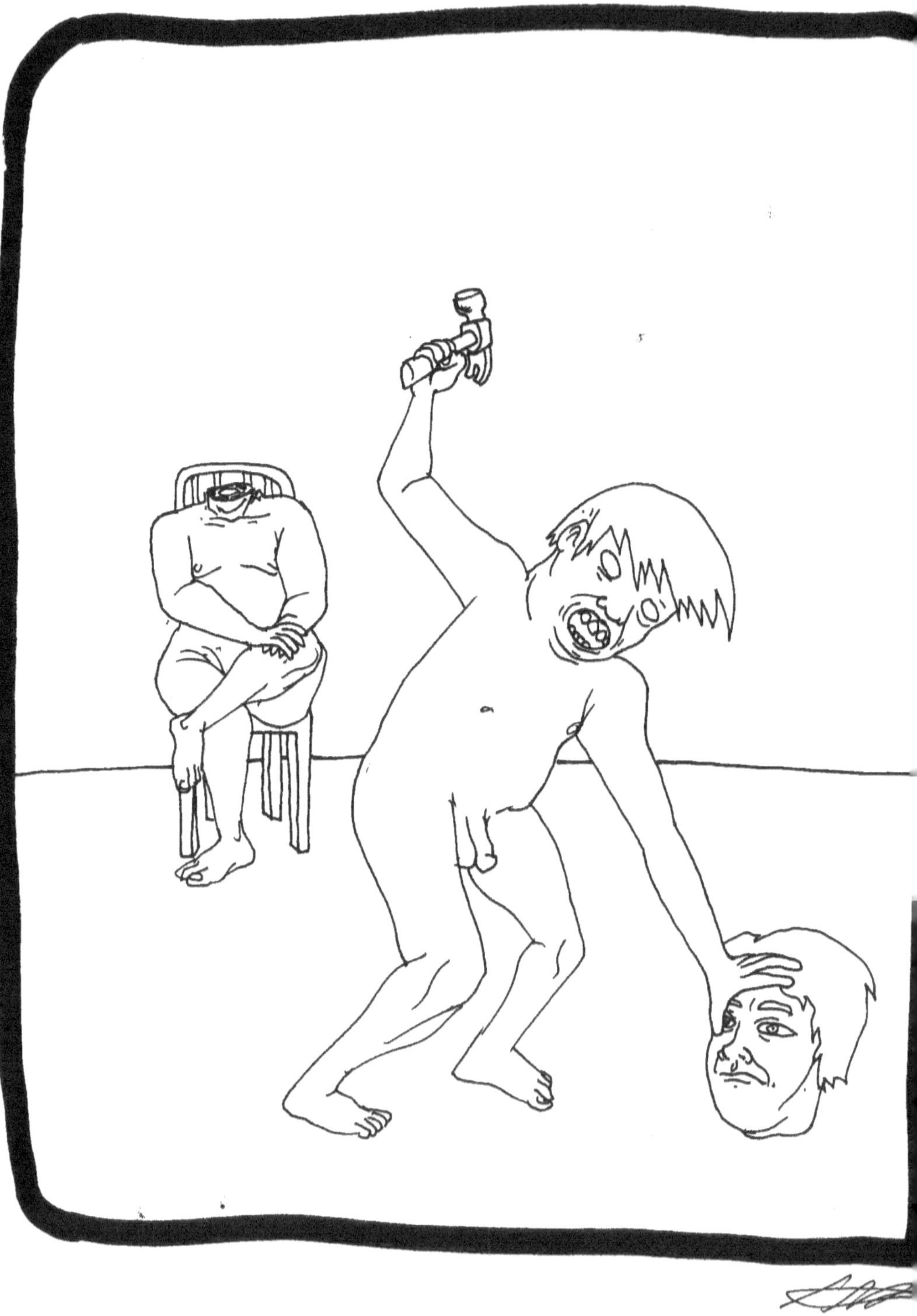

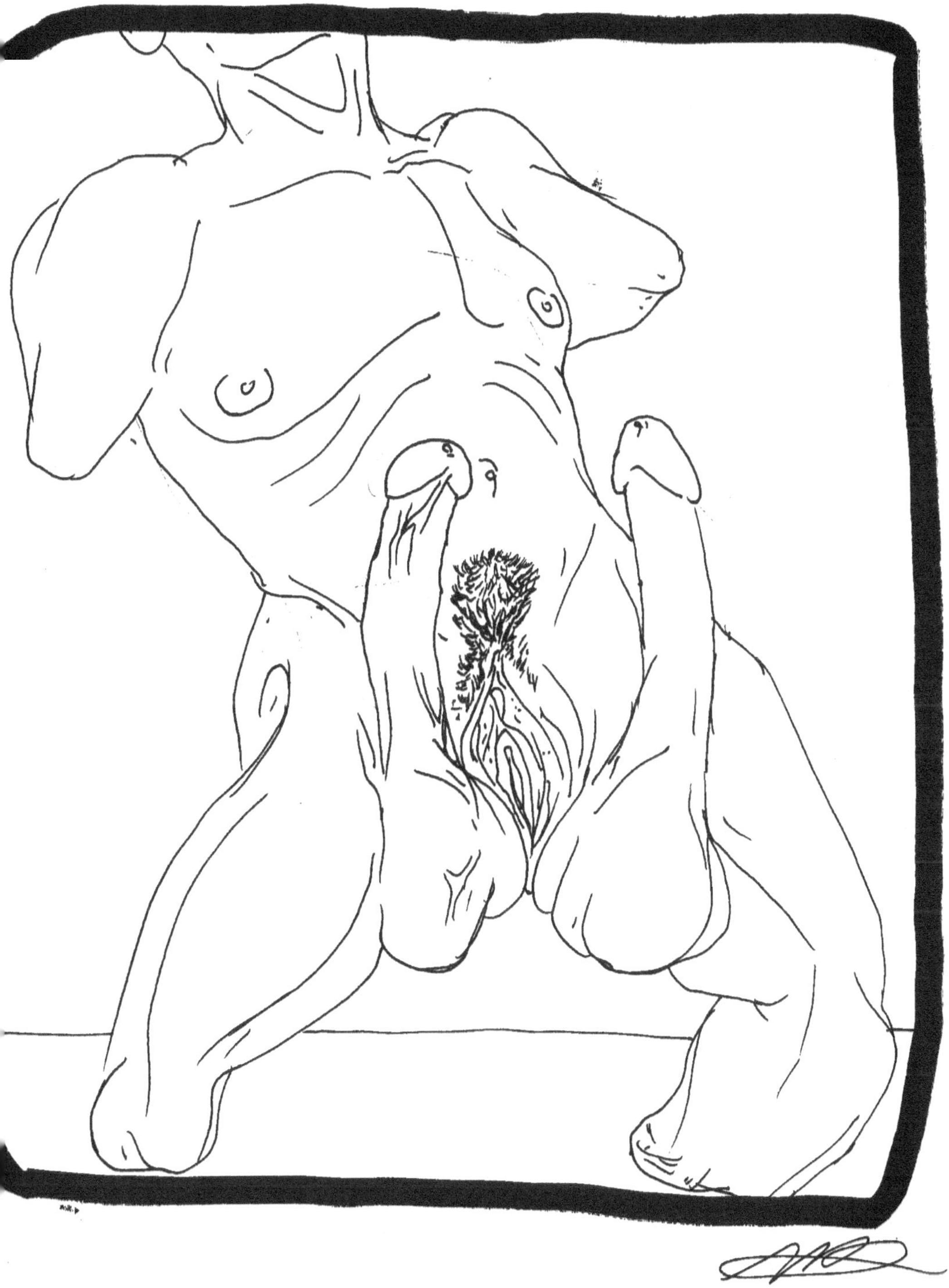

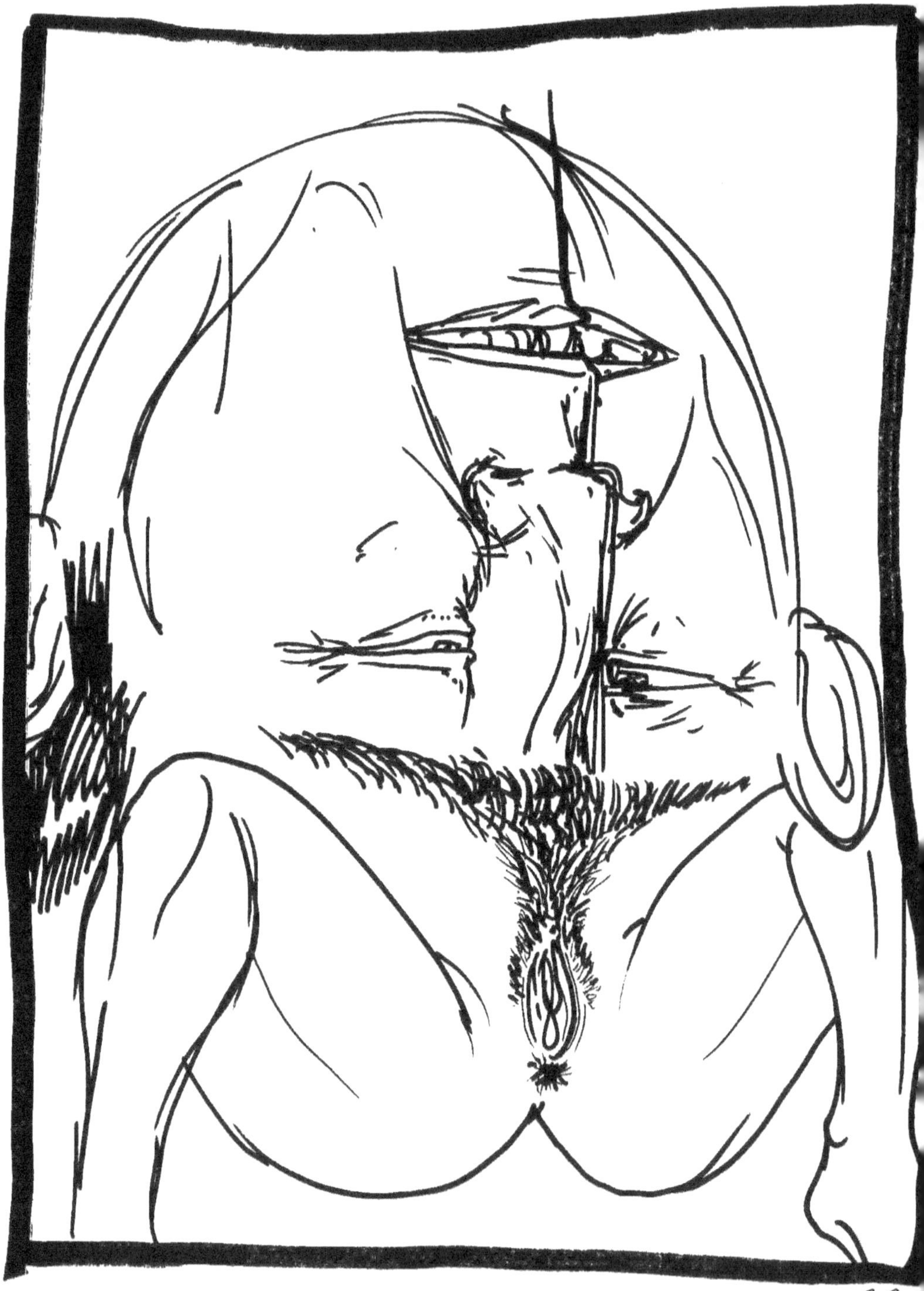

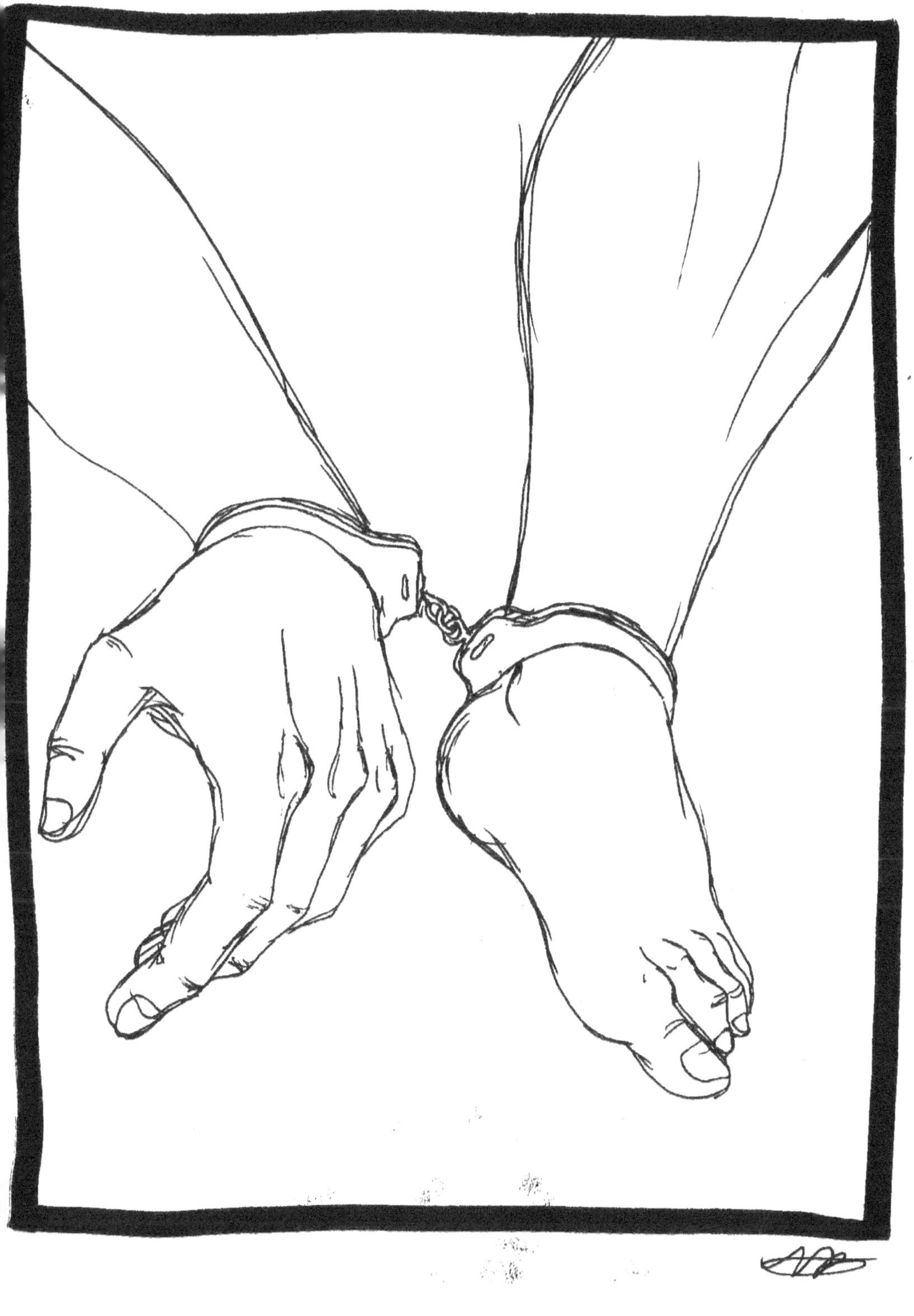

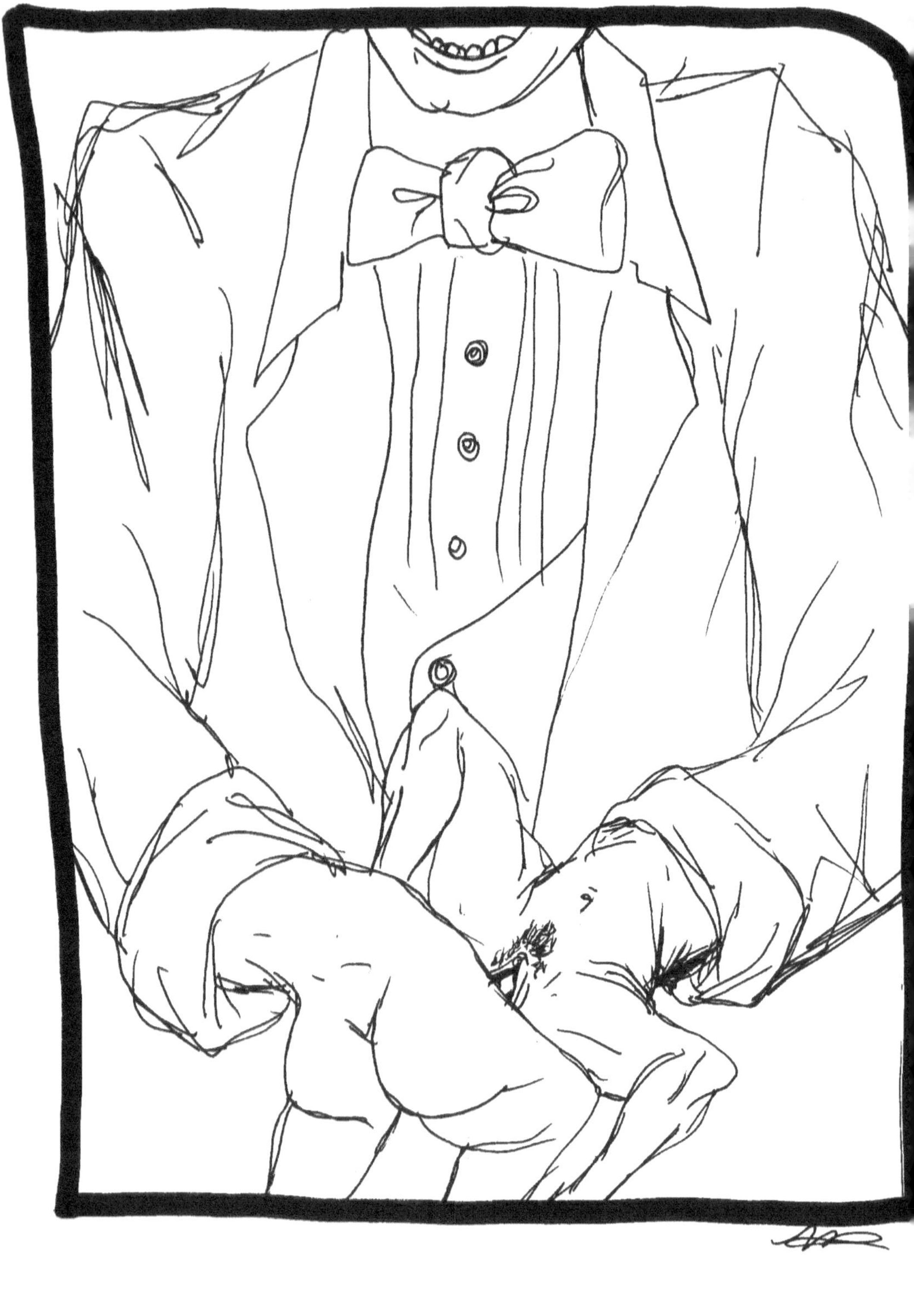

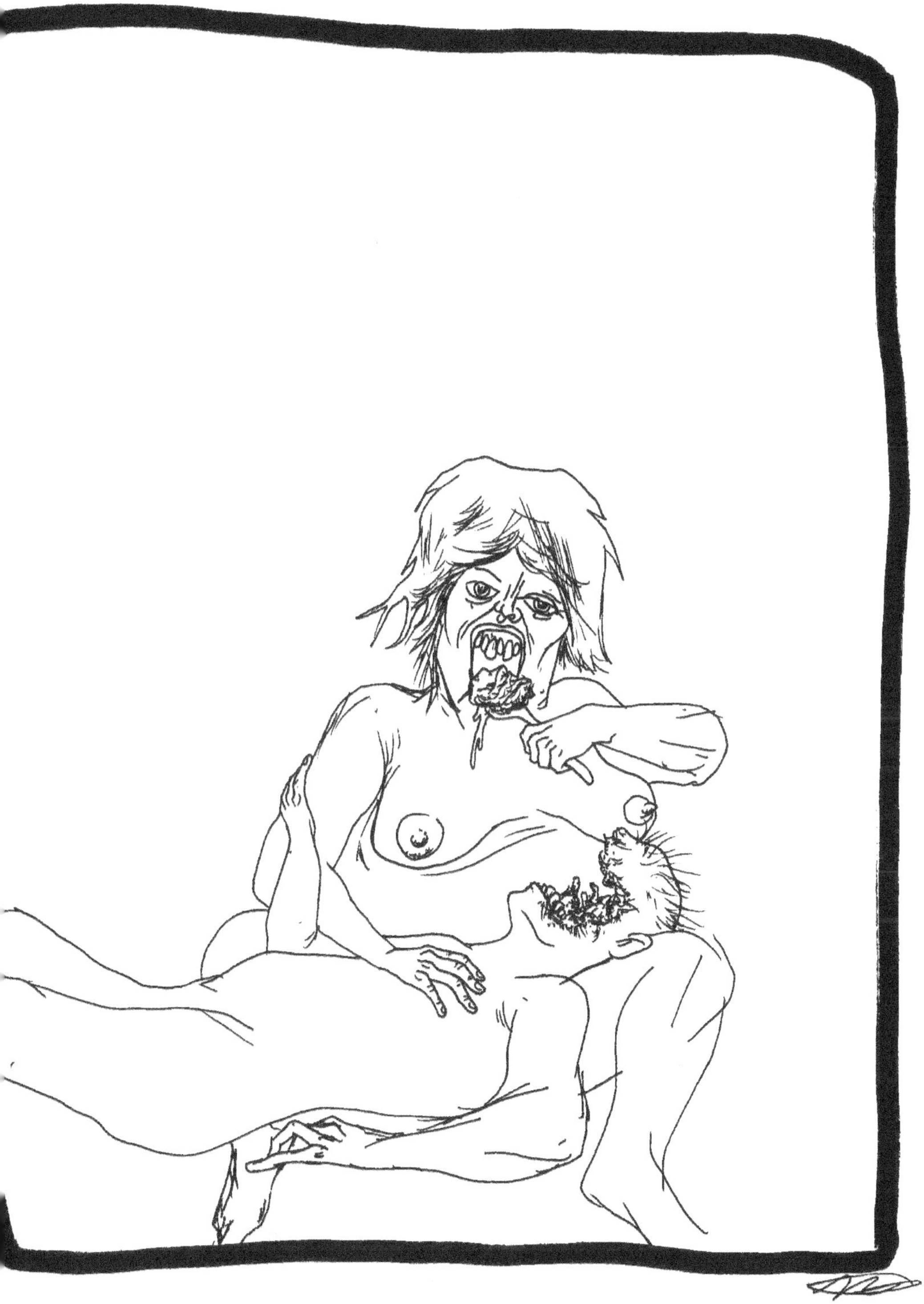

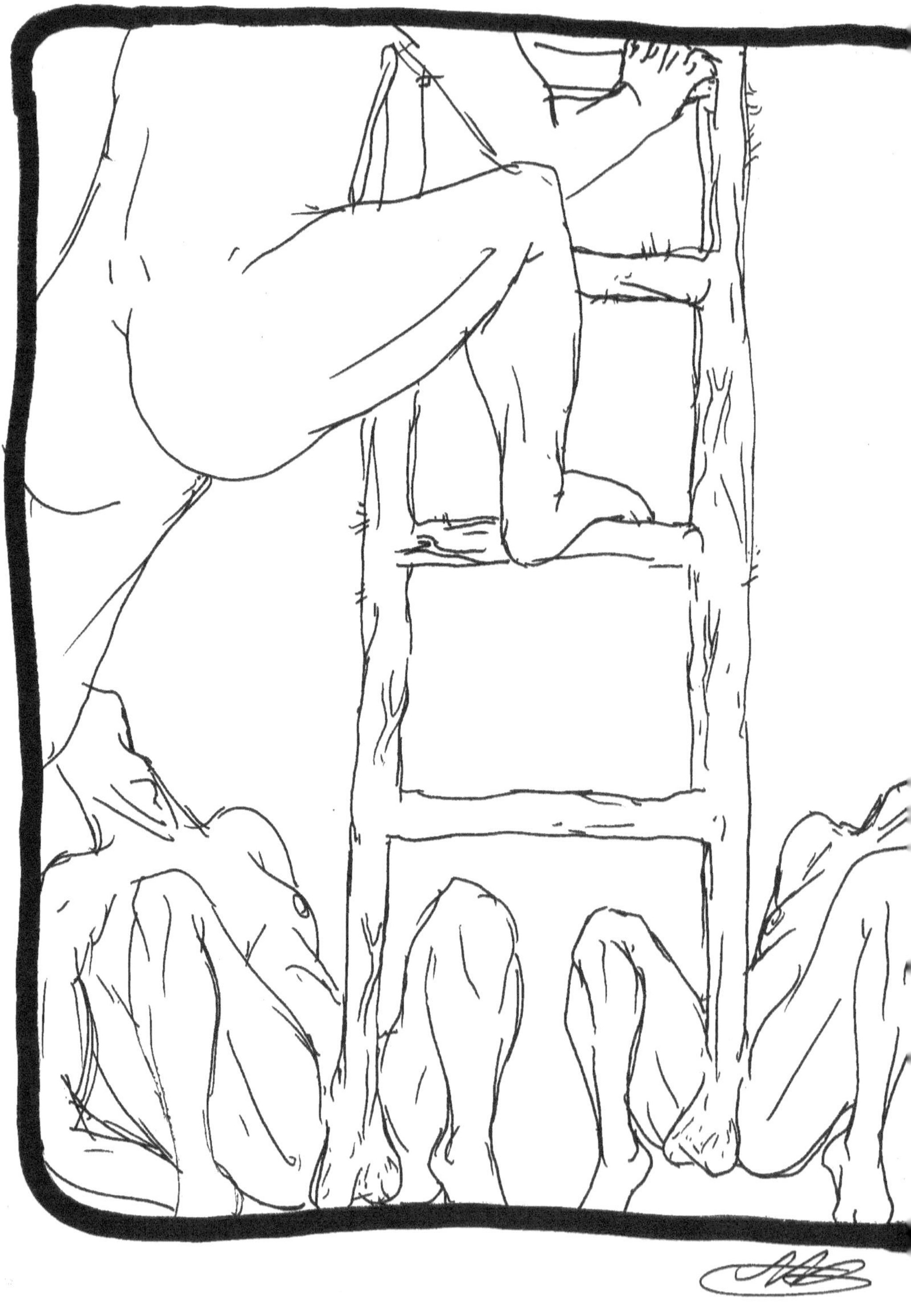

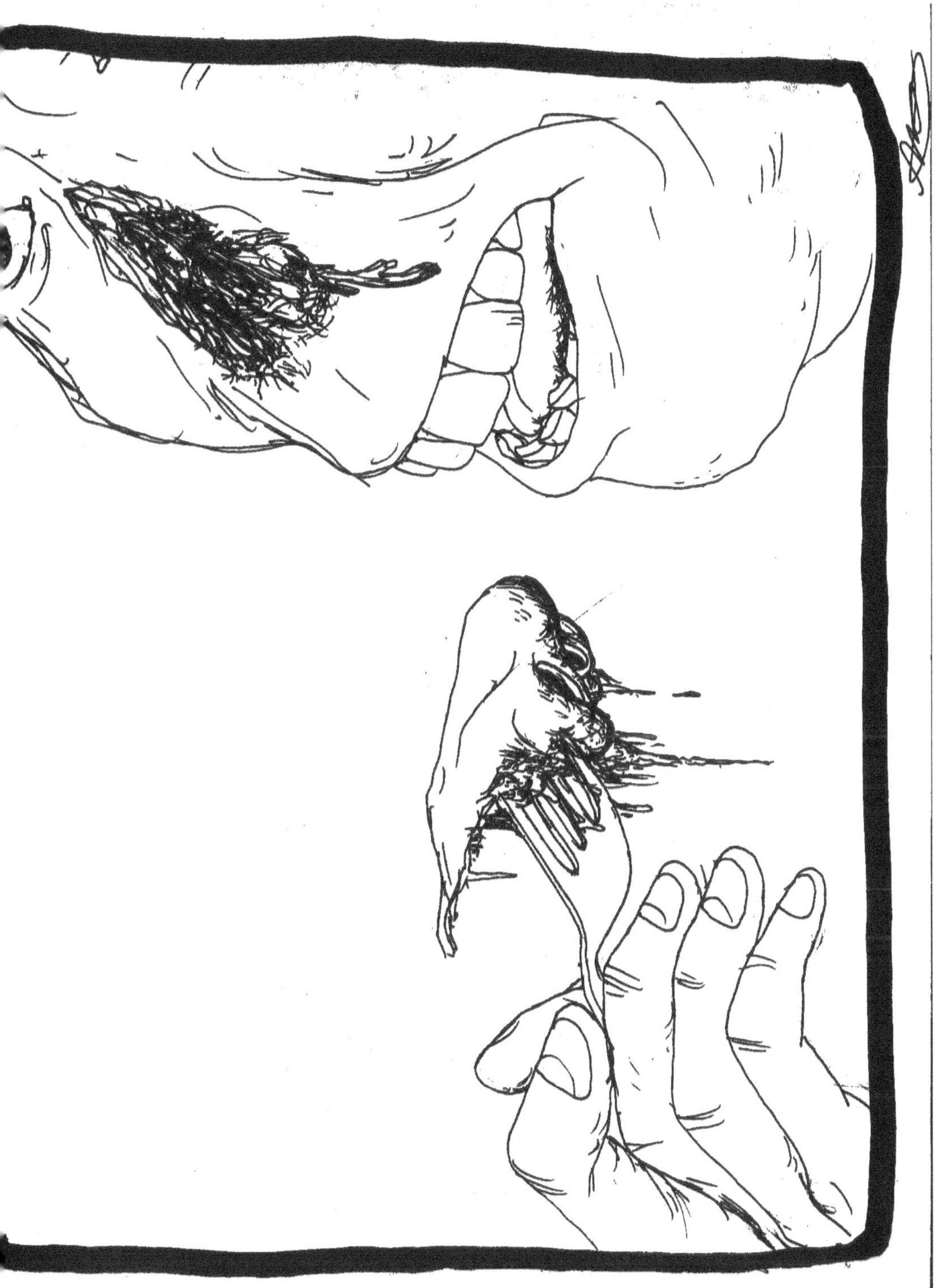

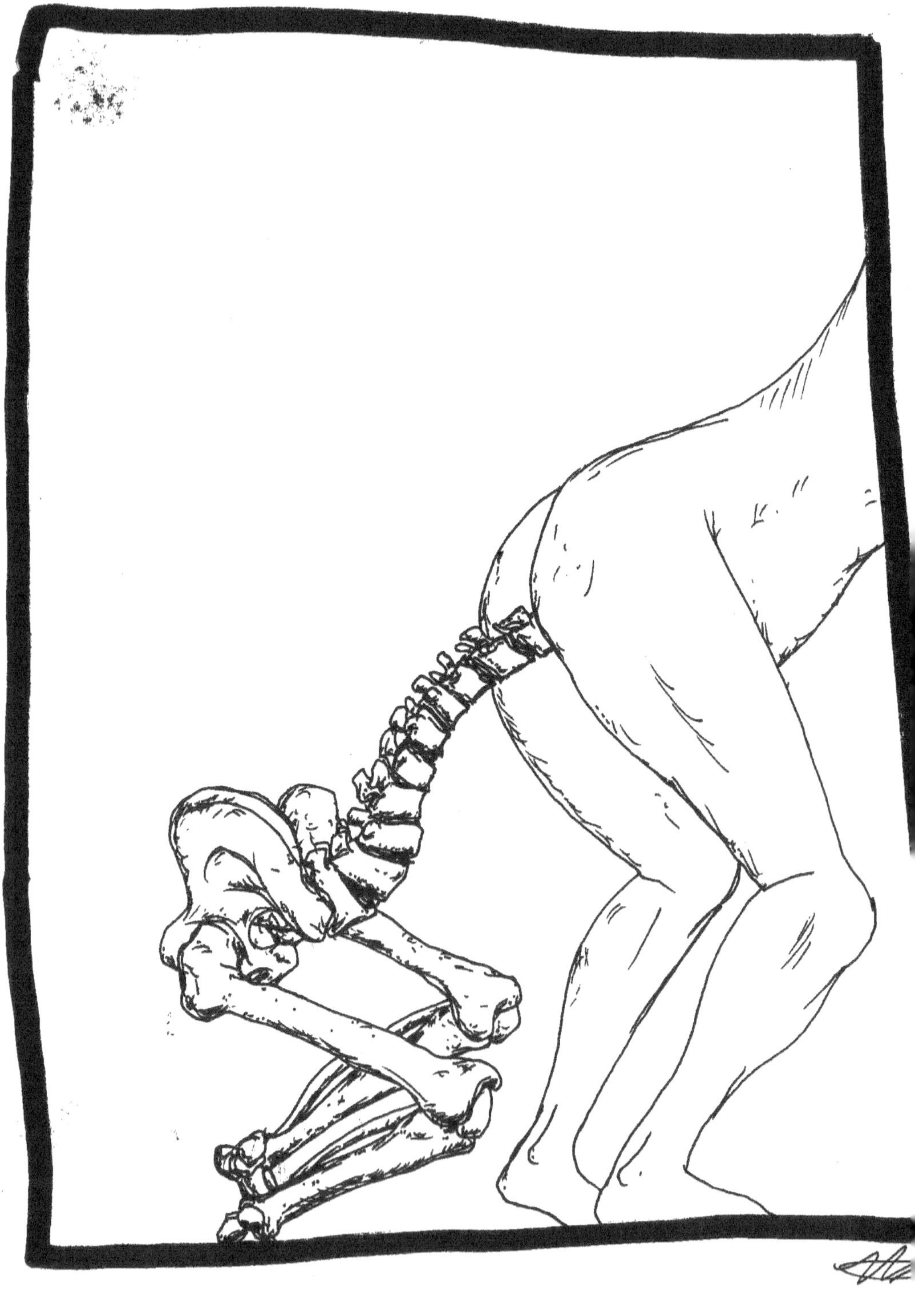

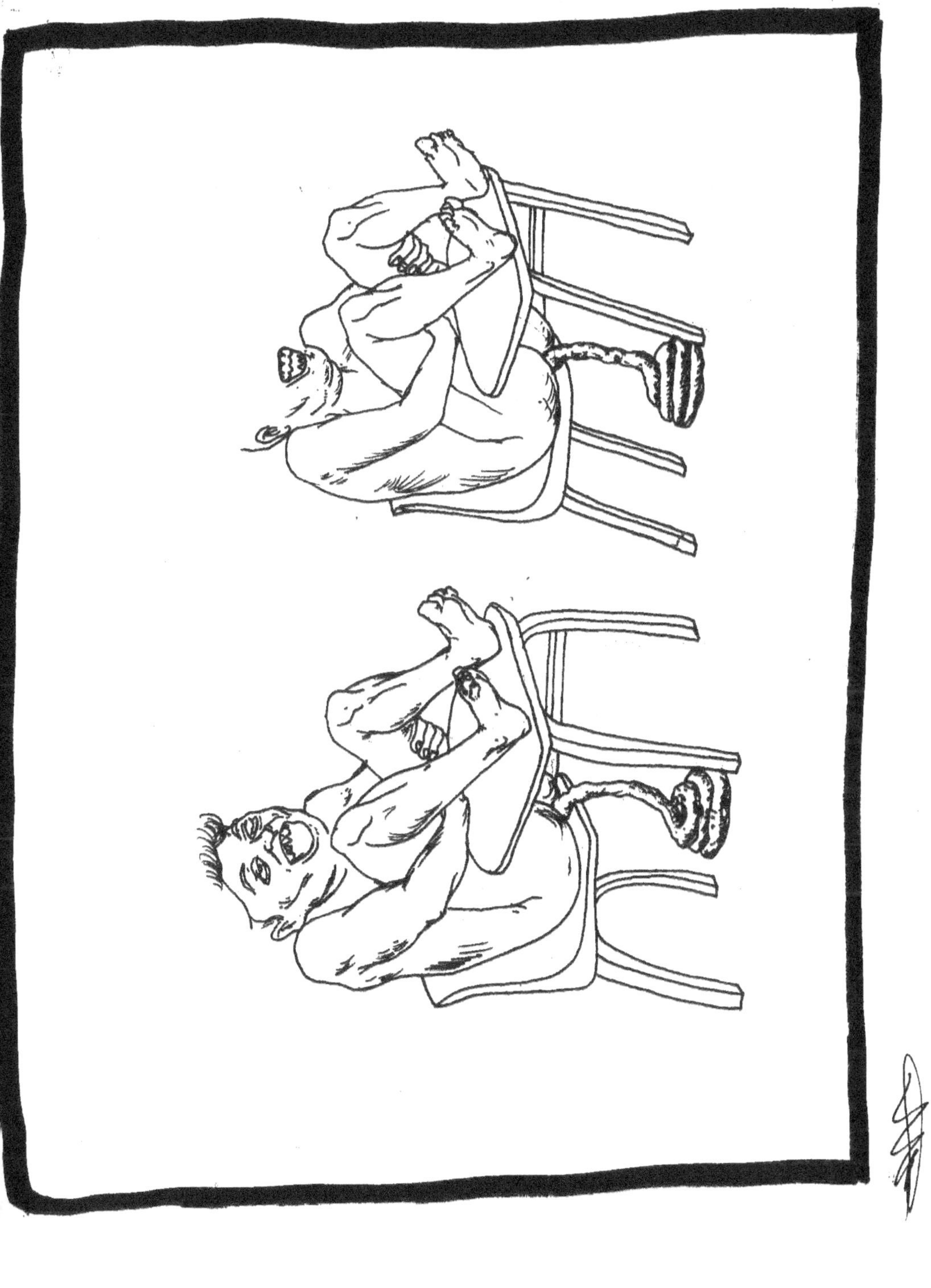

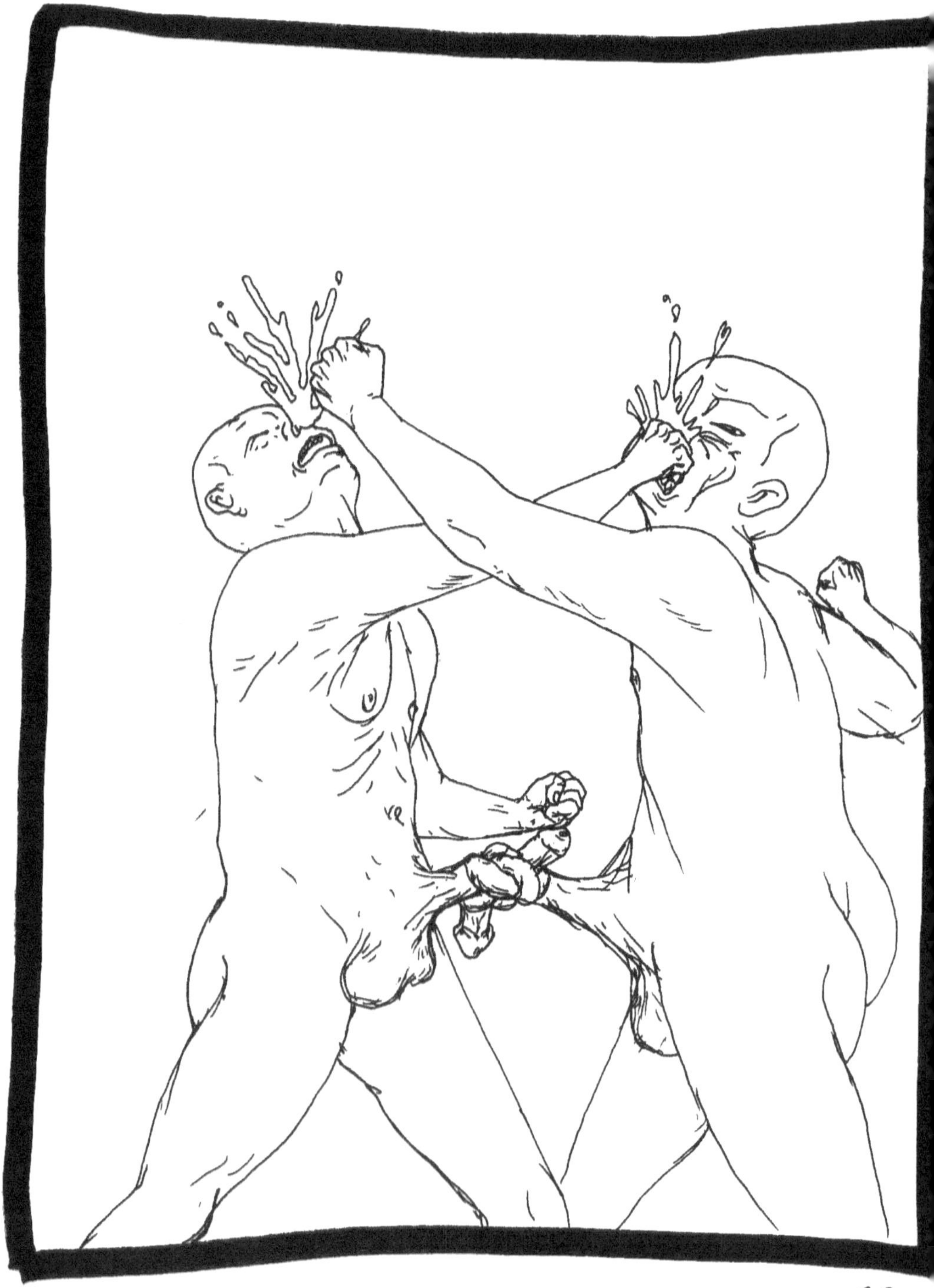

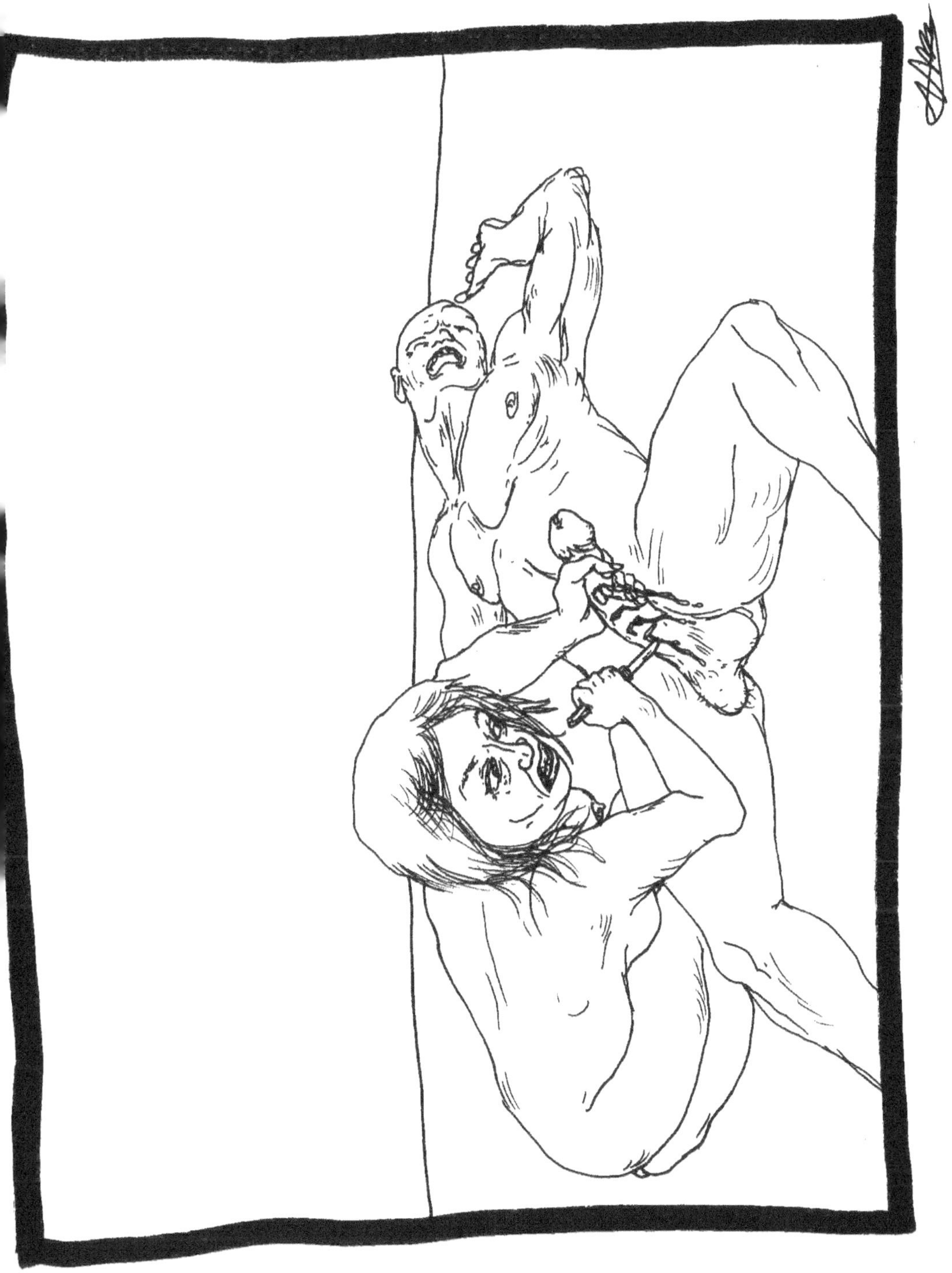

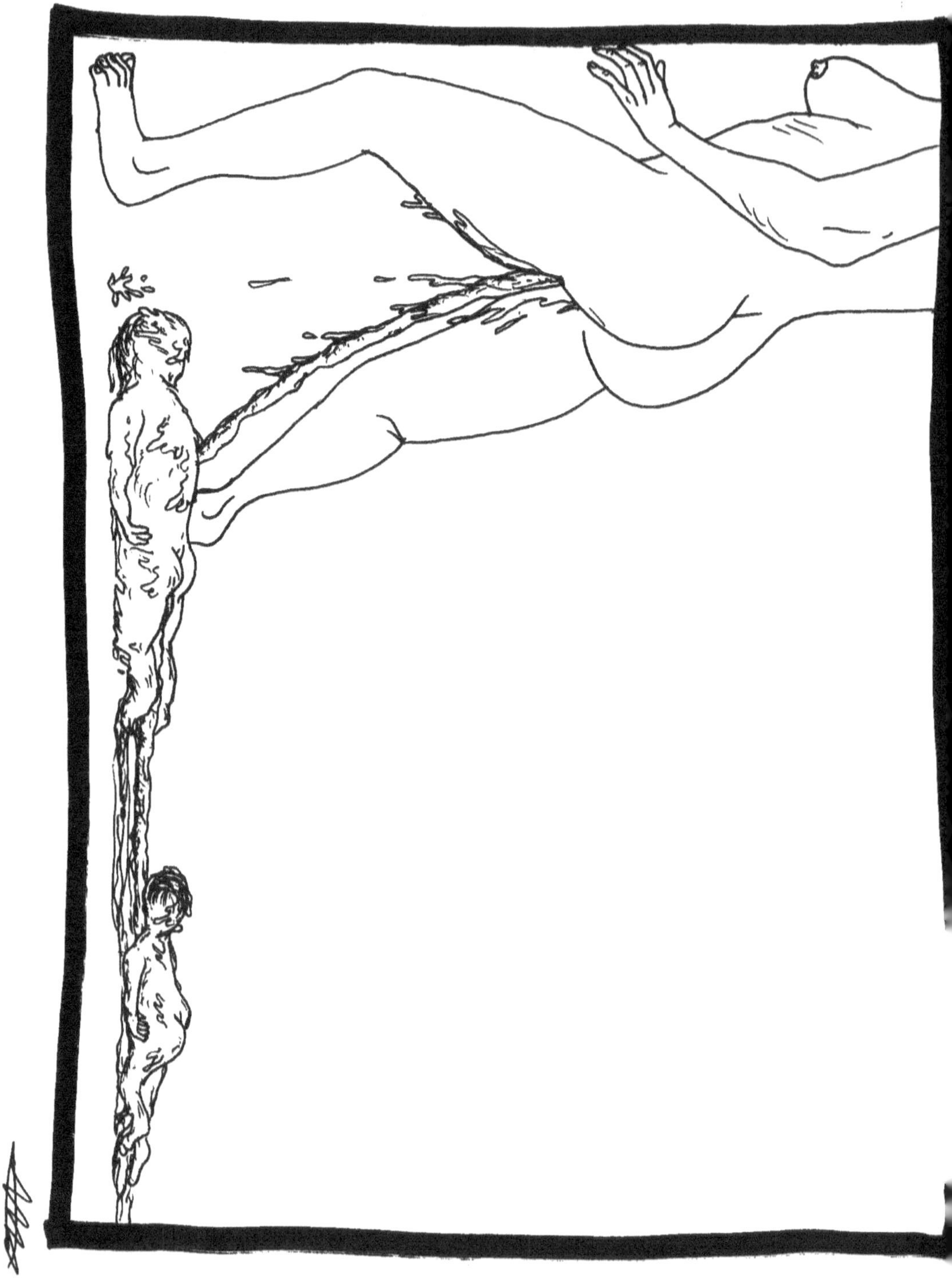

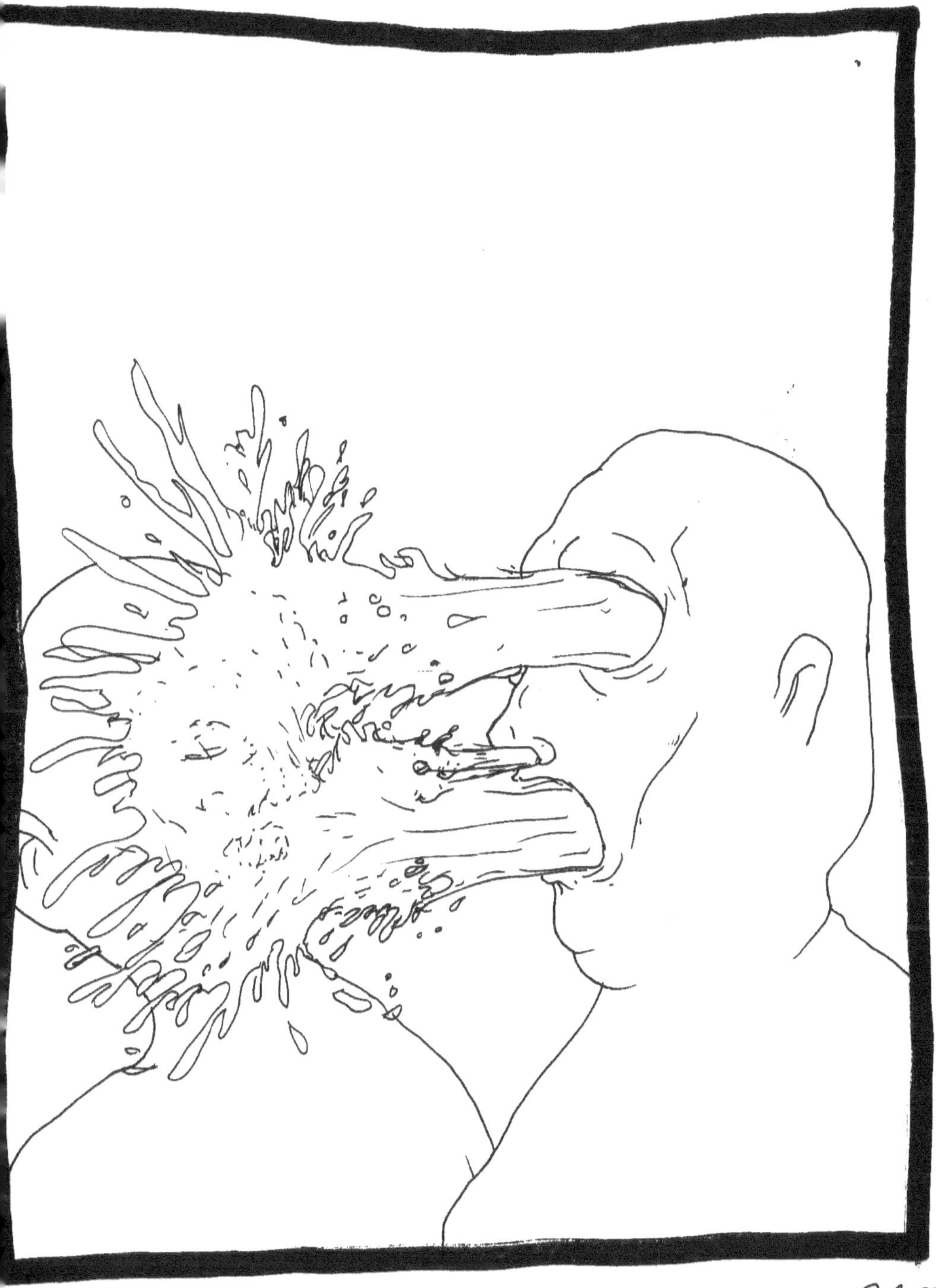

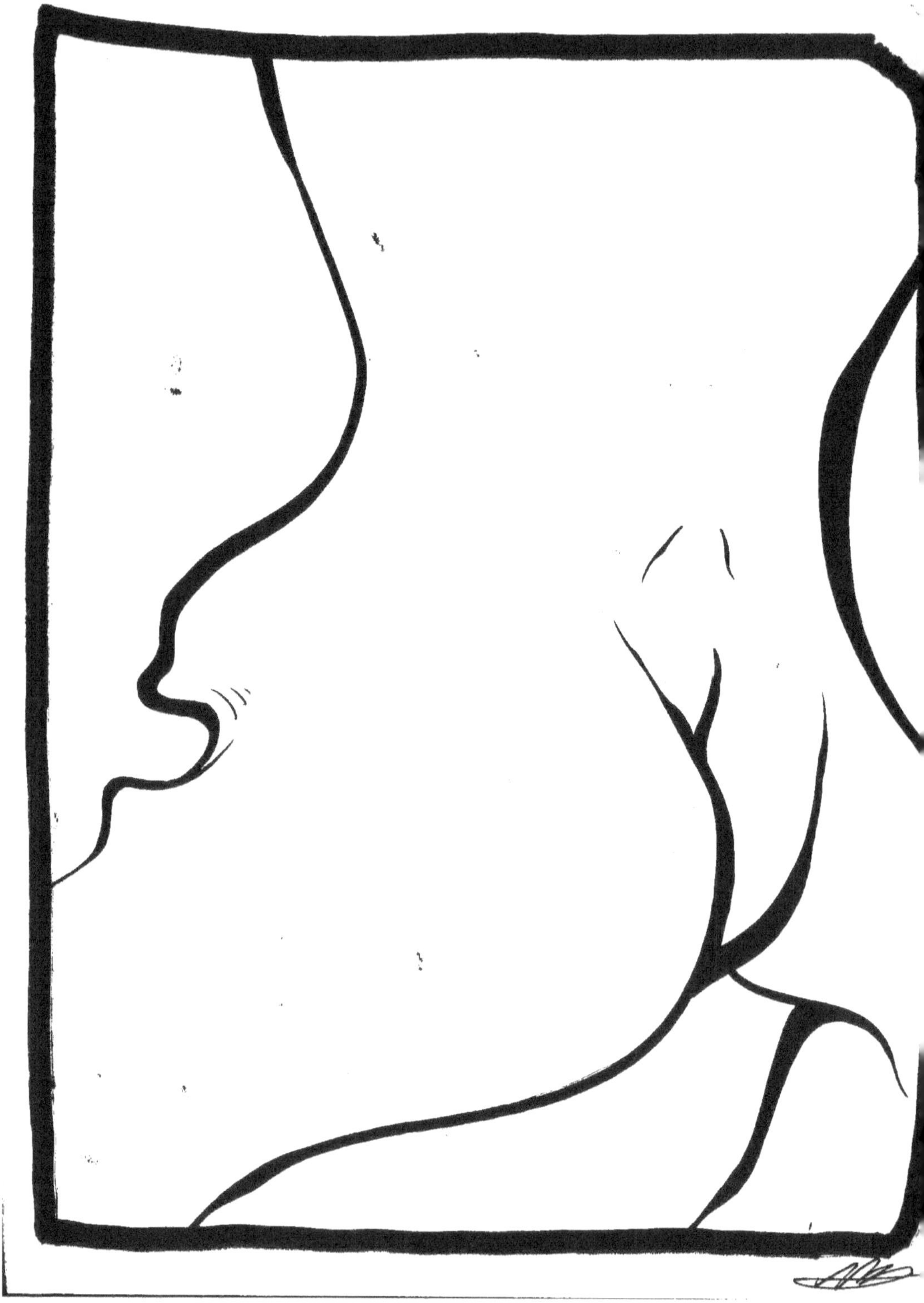

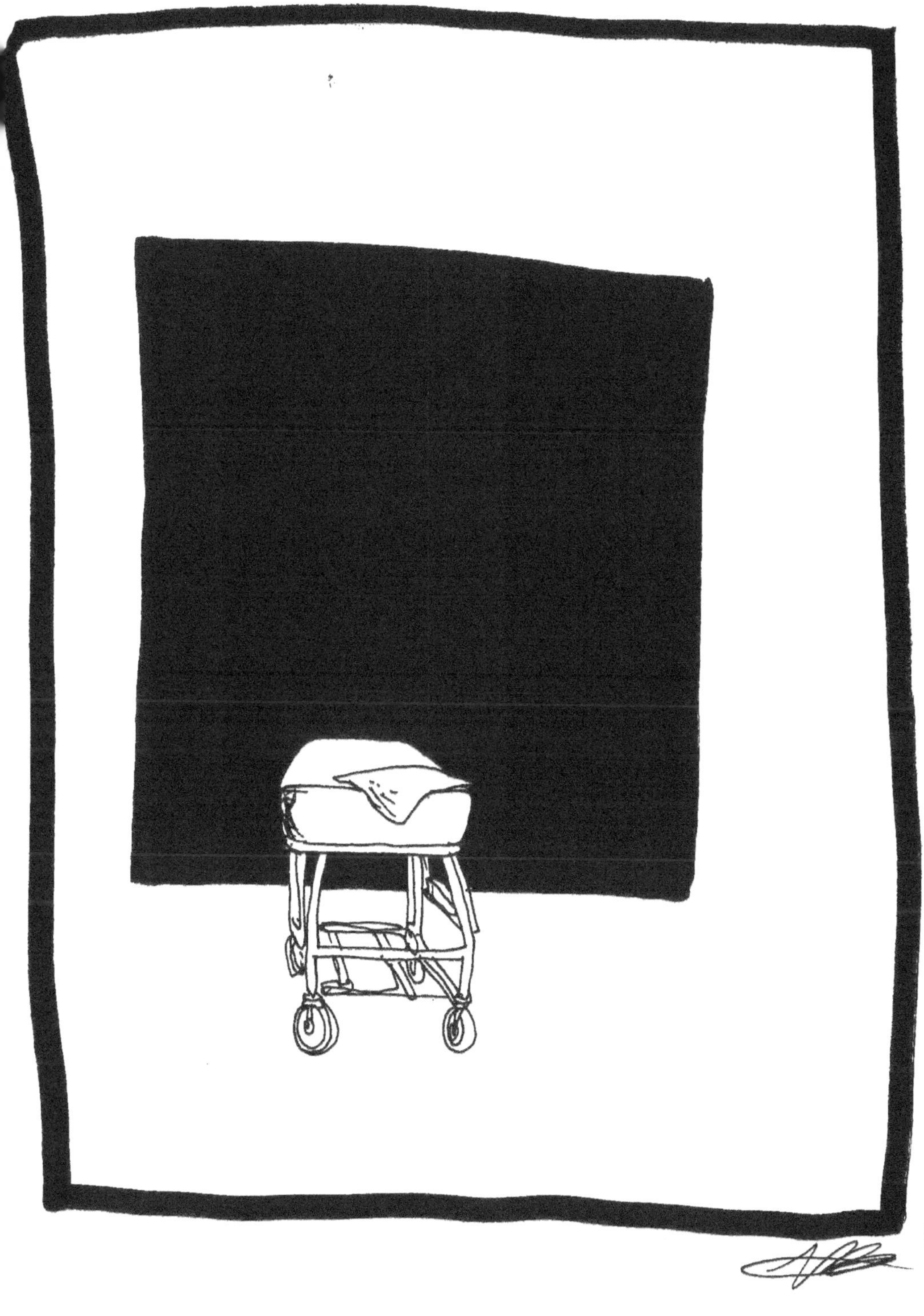

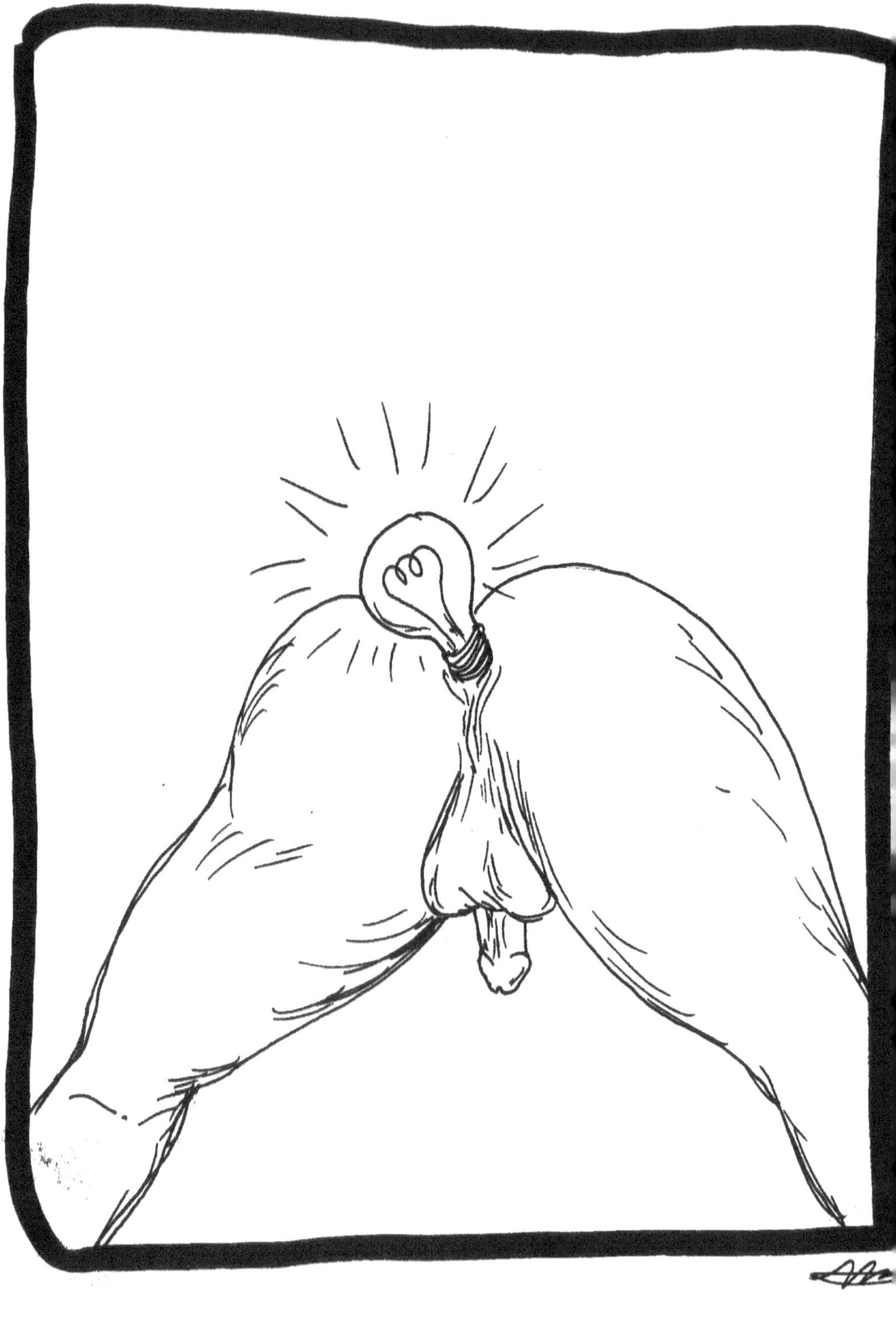

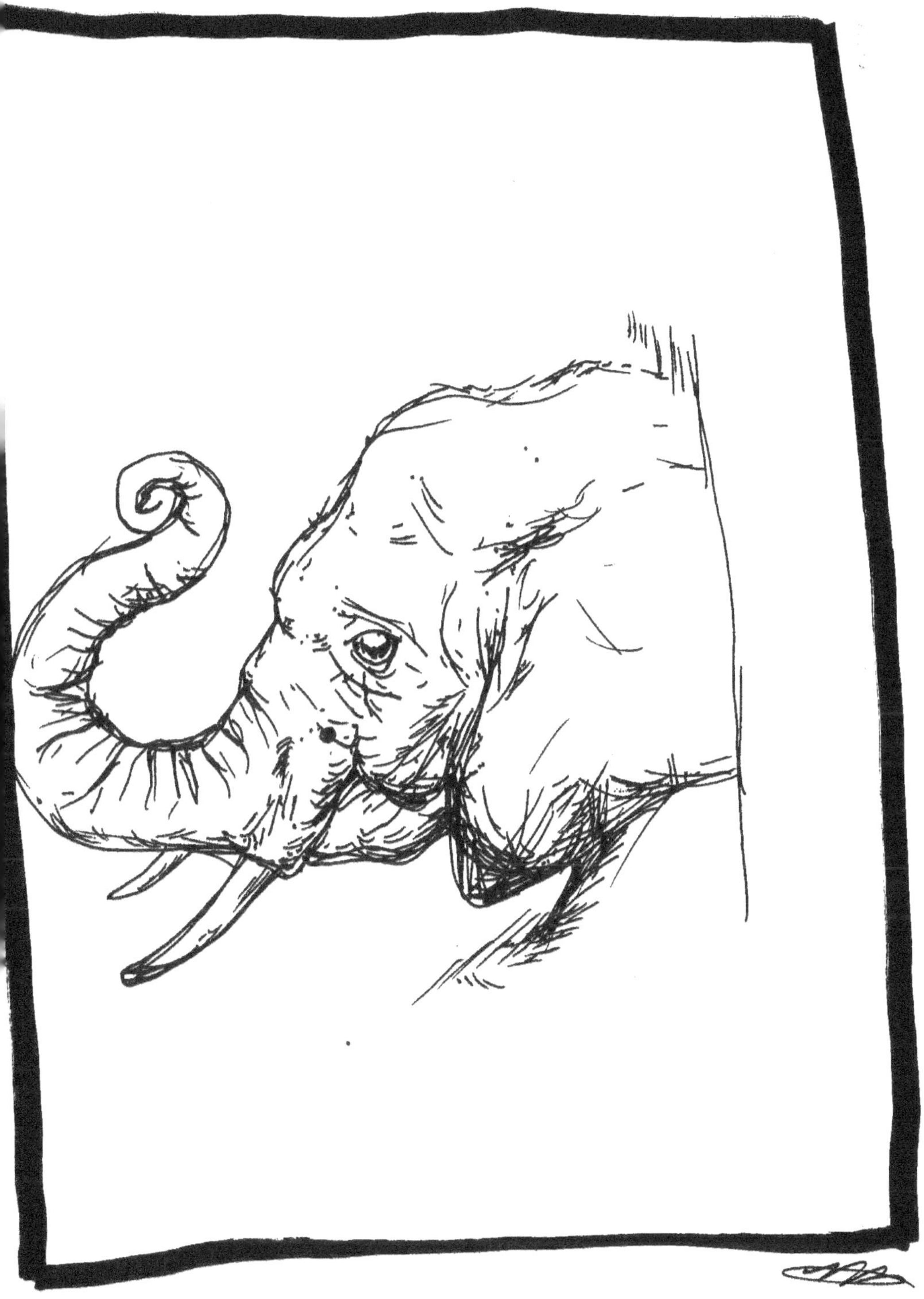

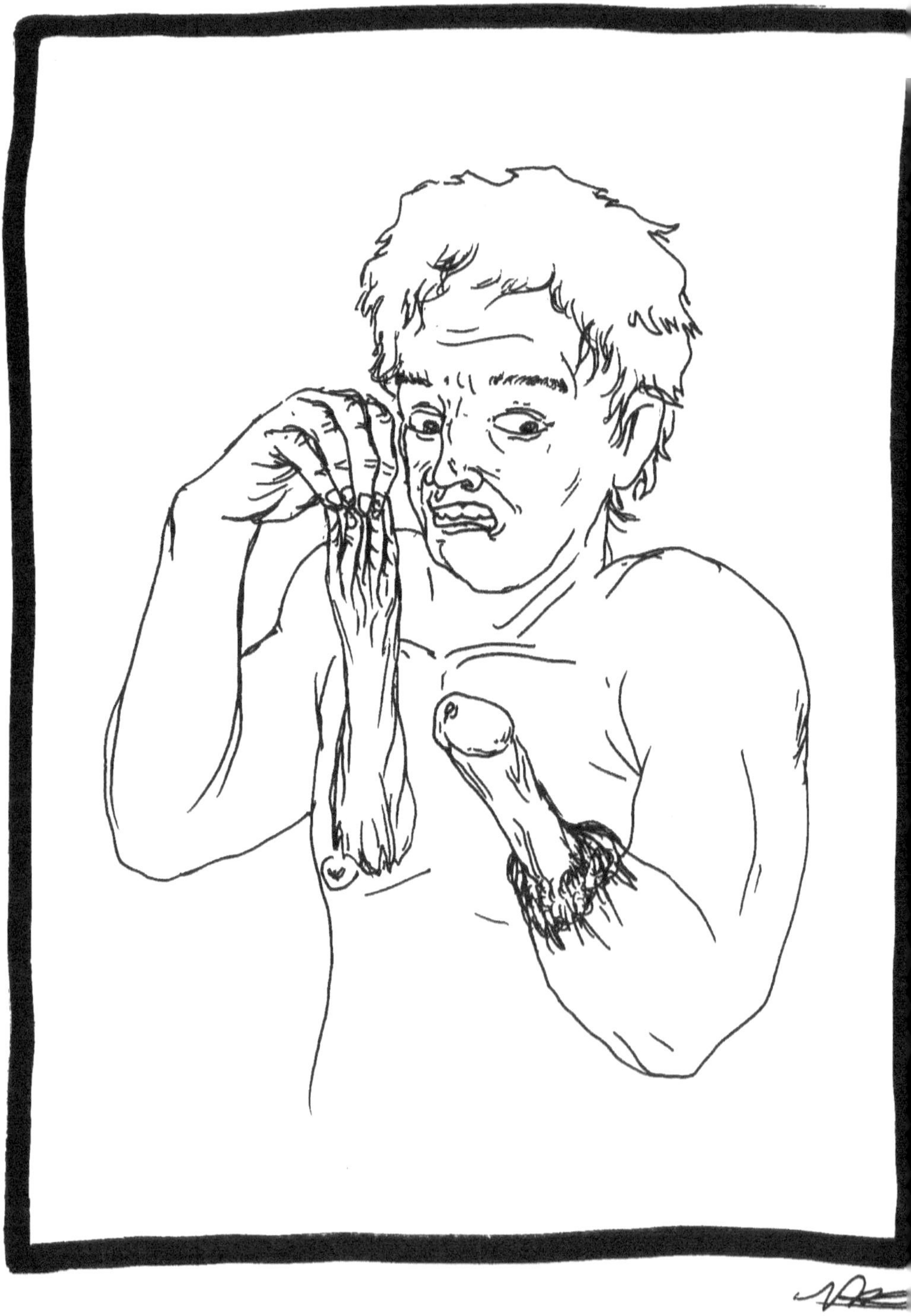

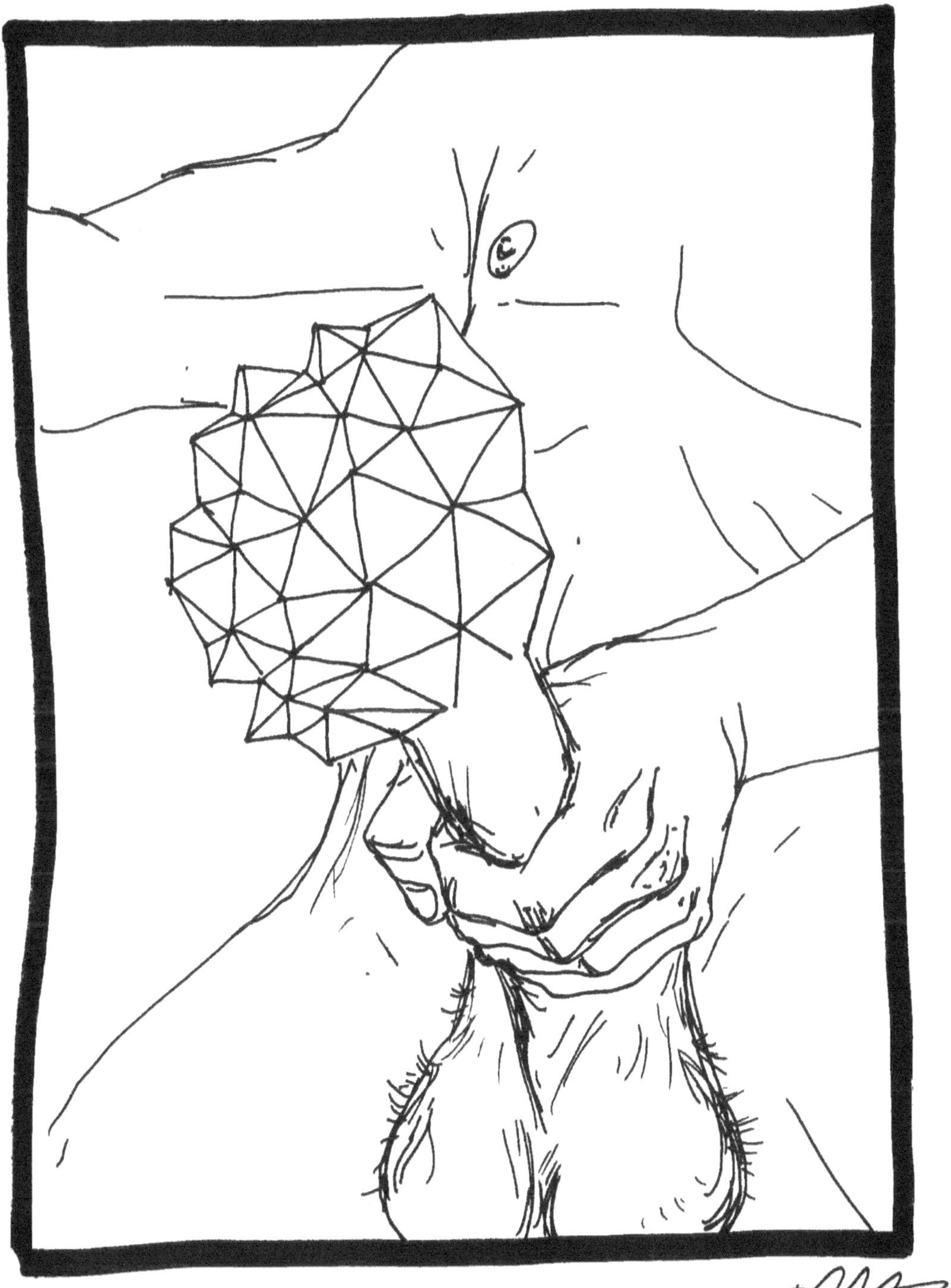

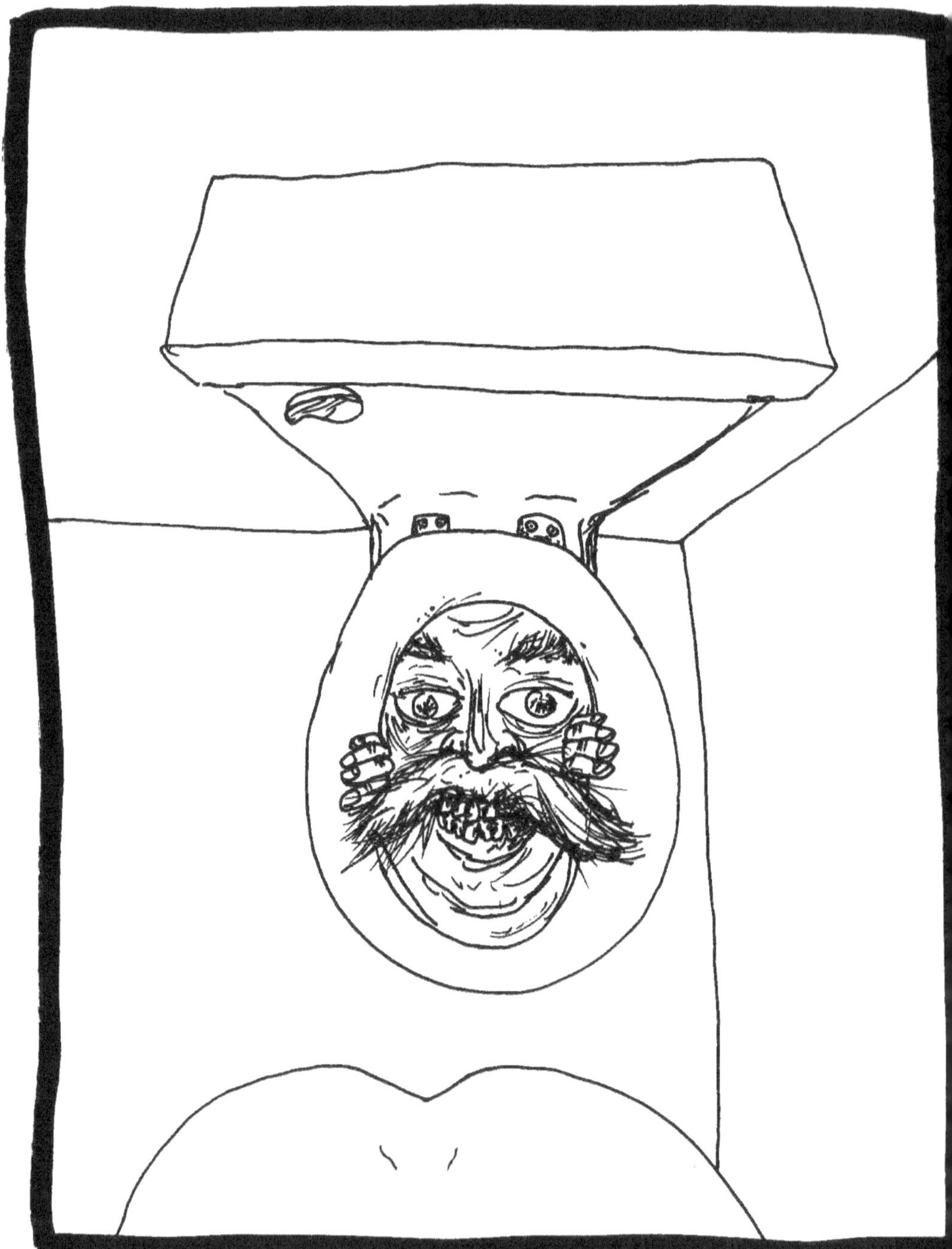

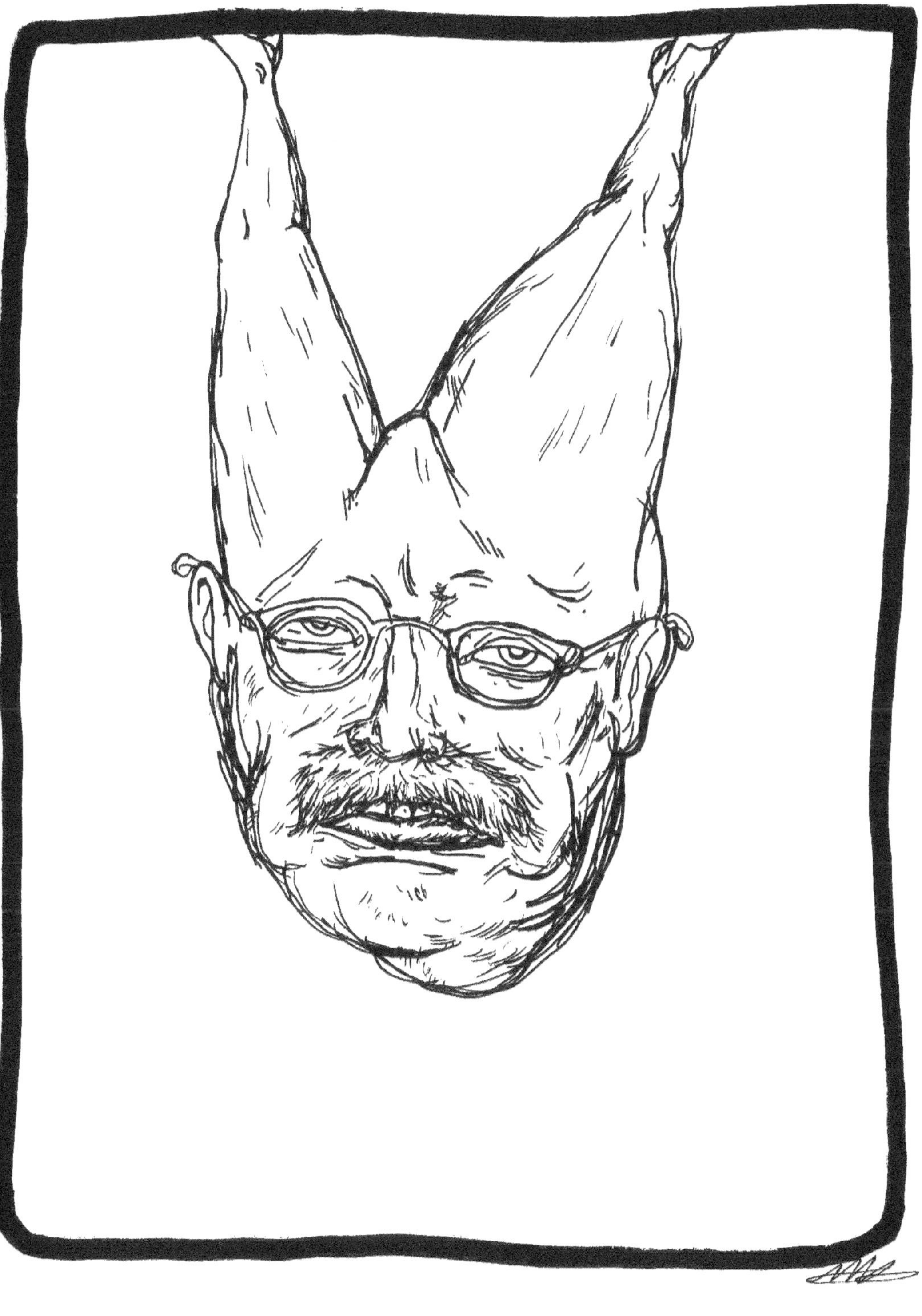

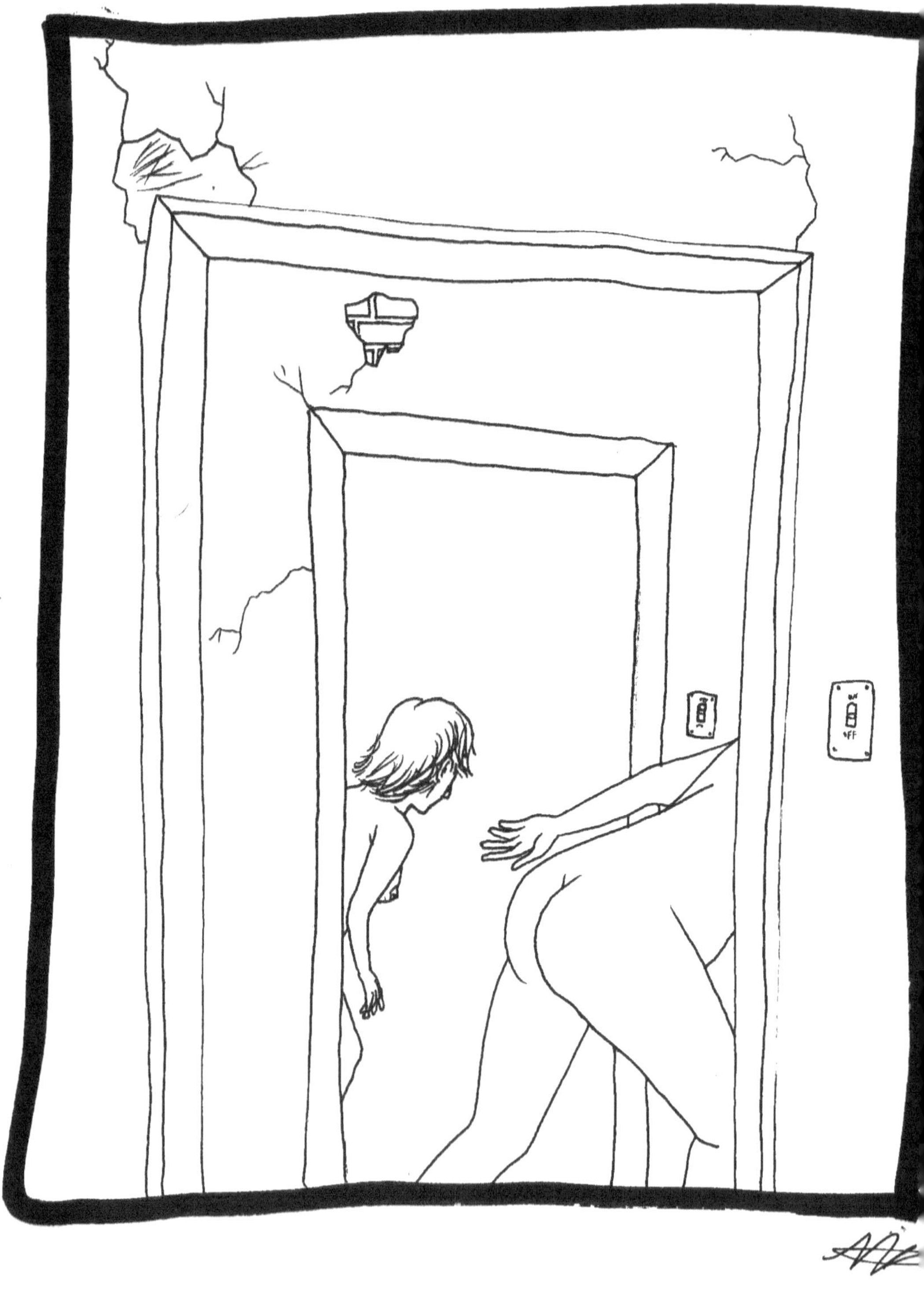

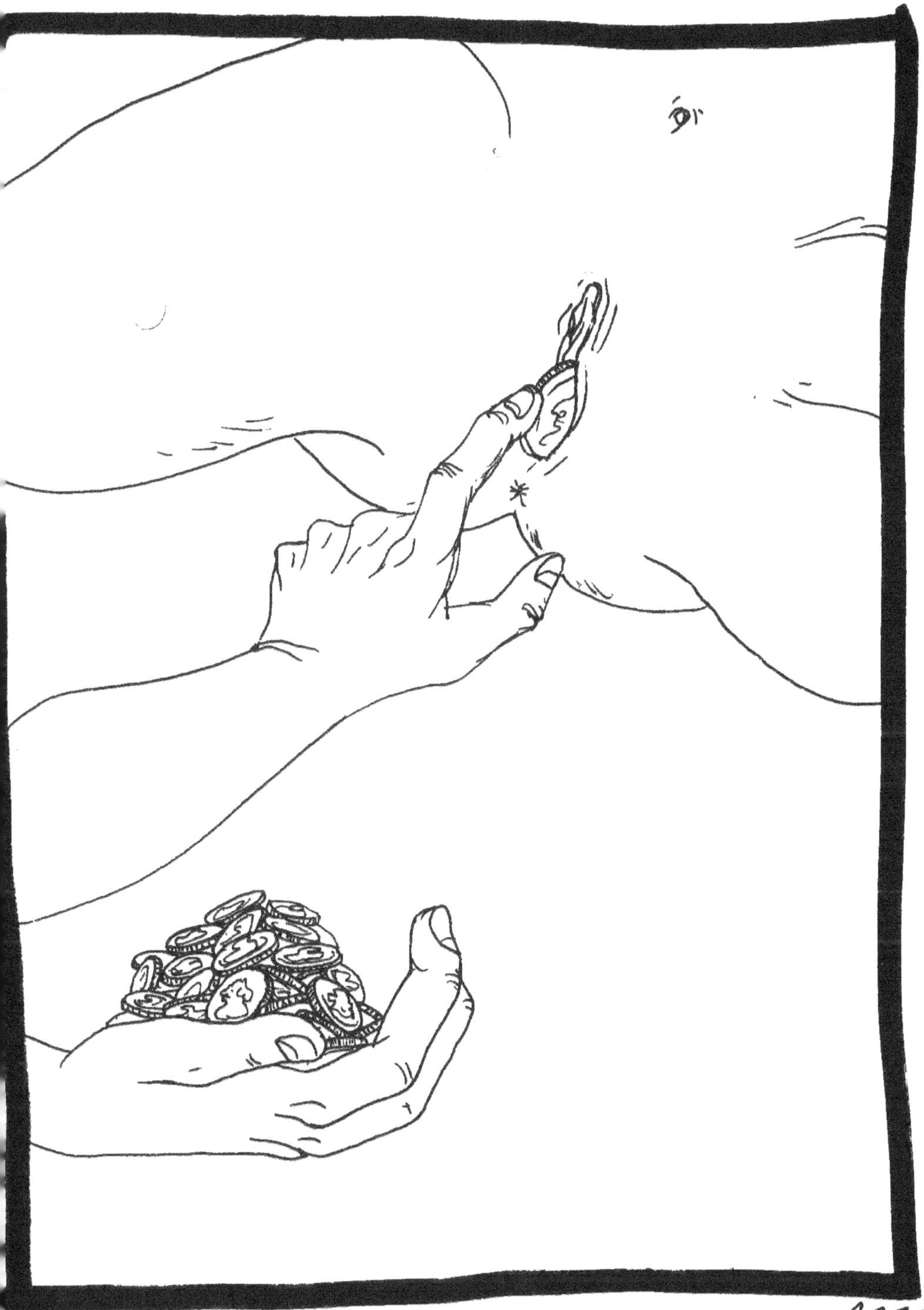

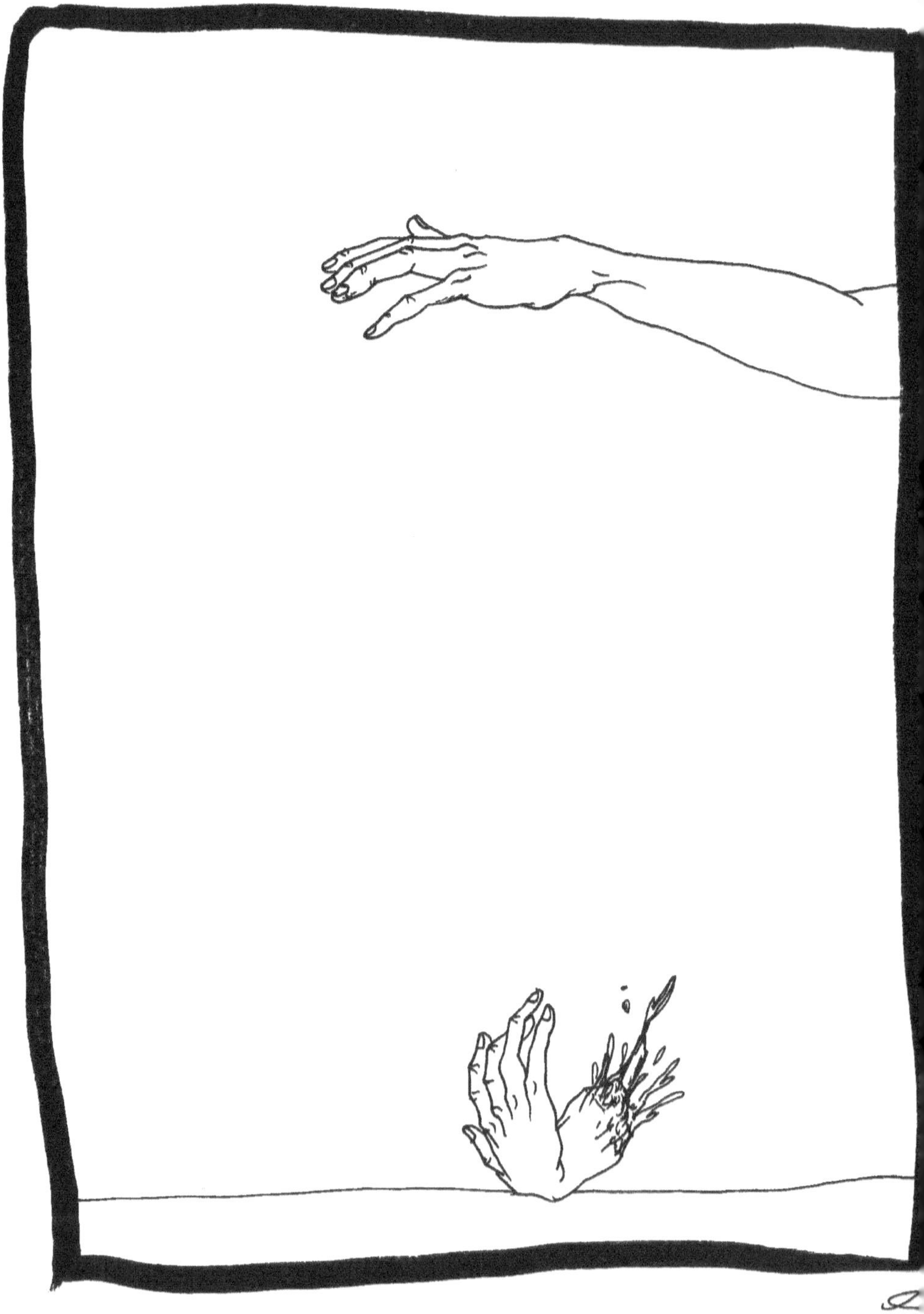

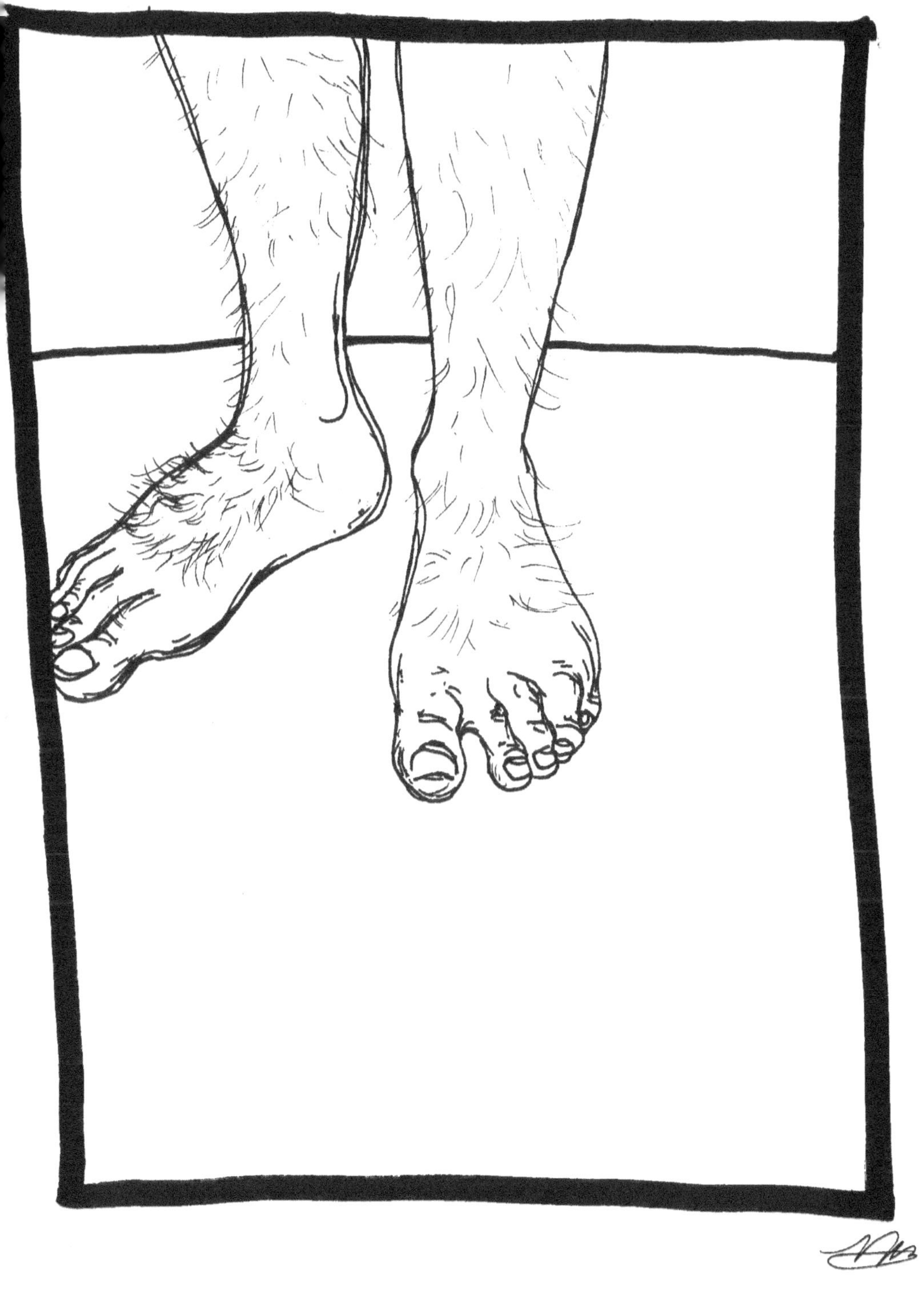

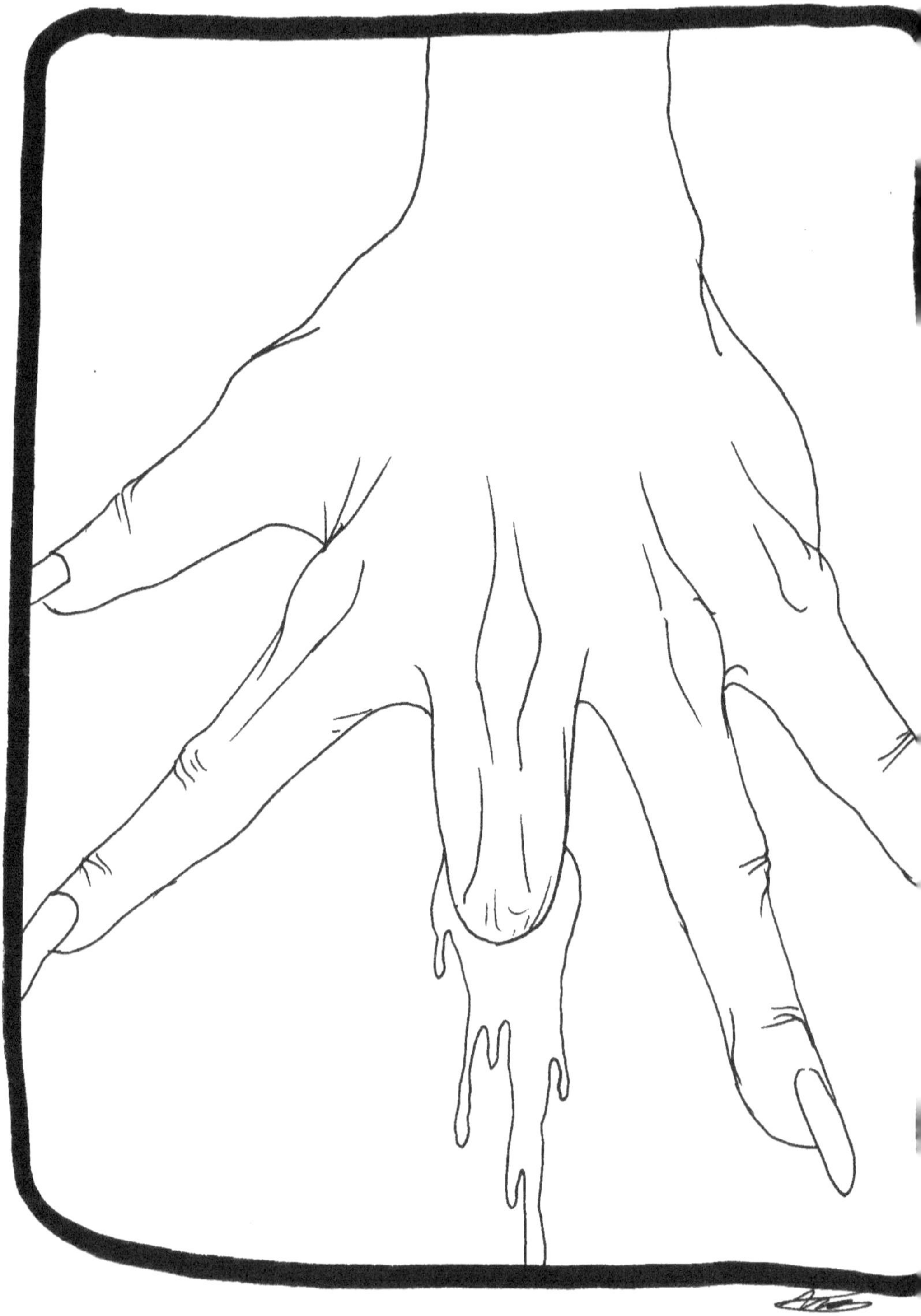

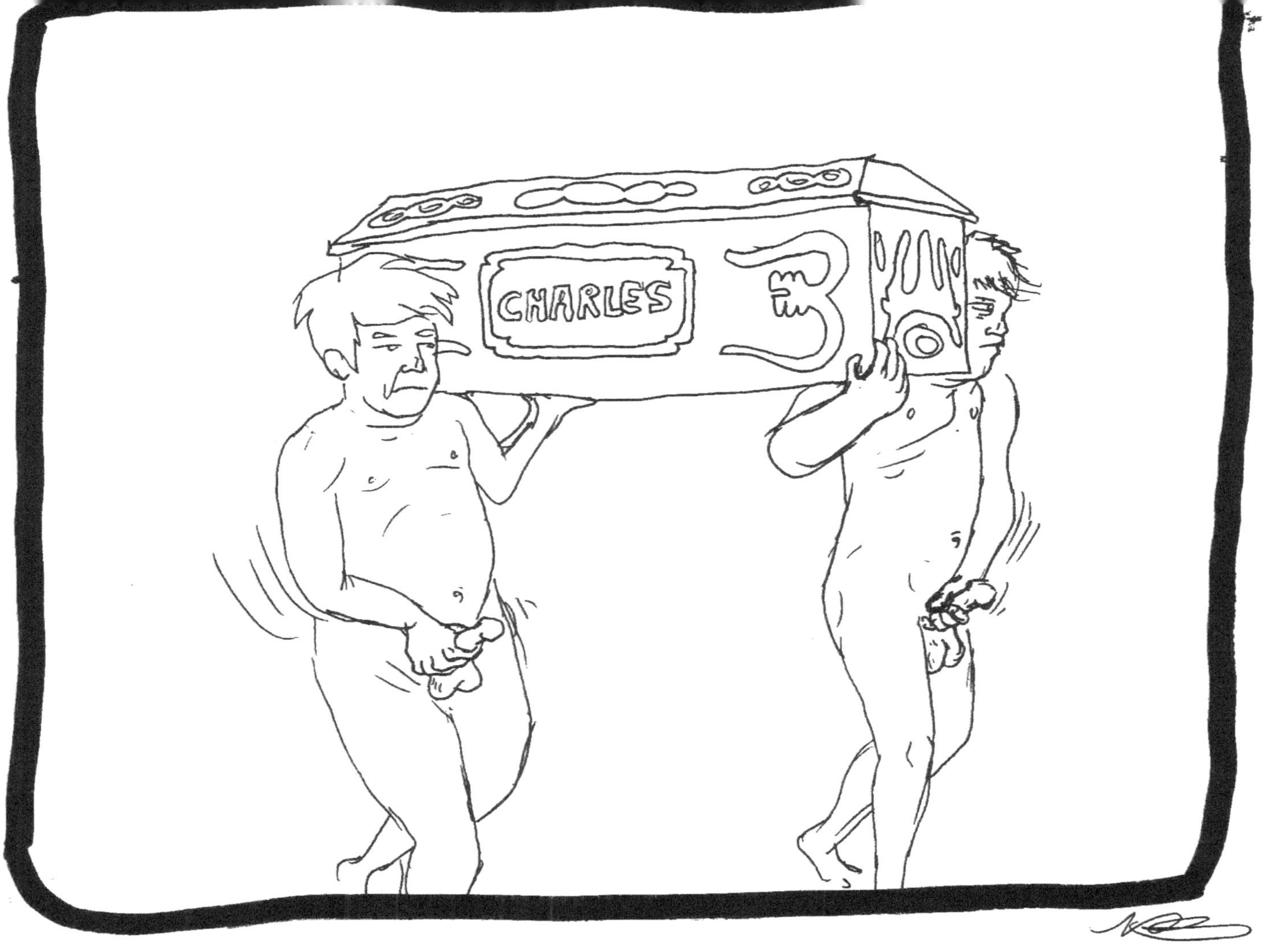
CHARLES

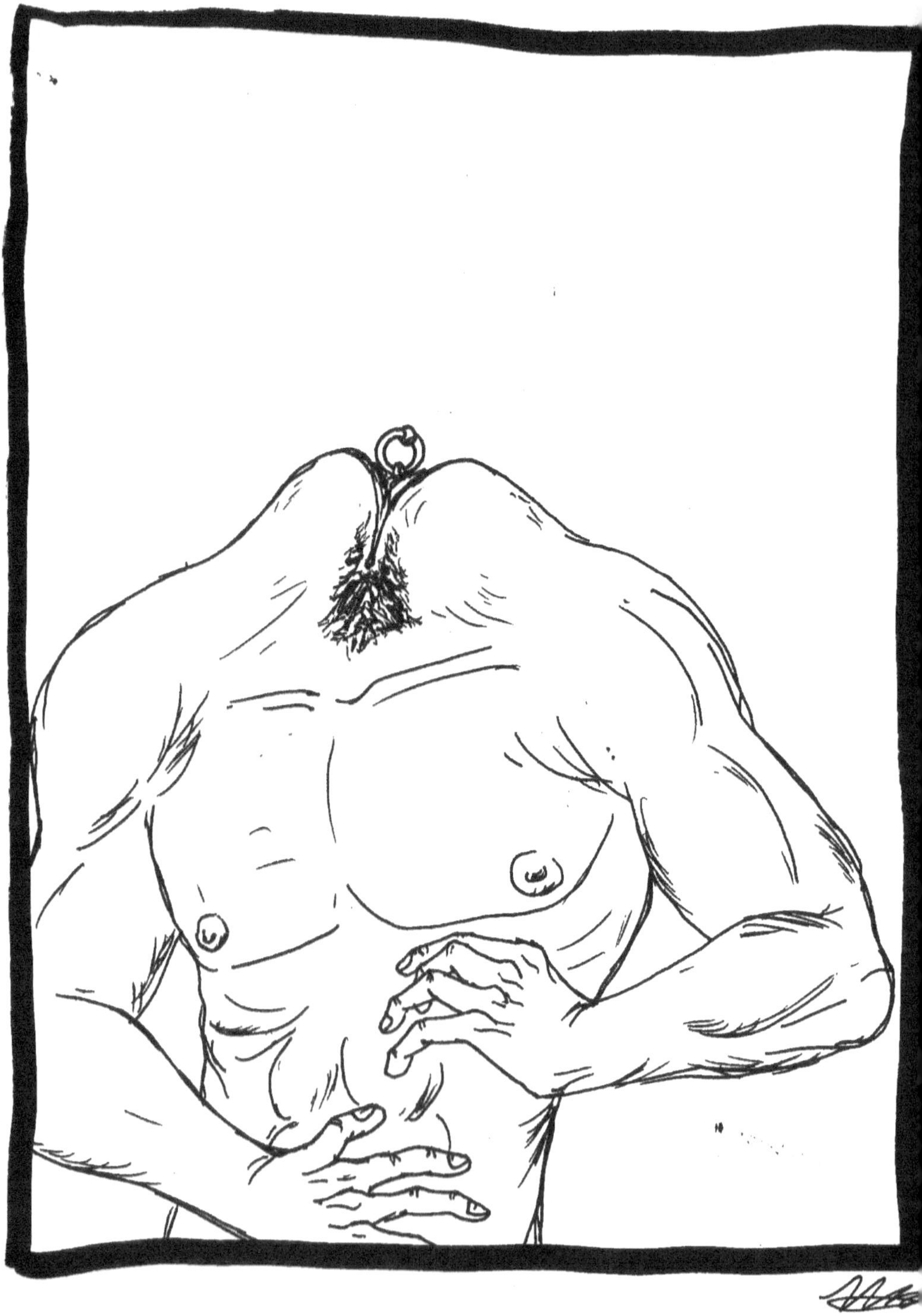

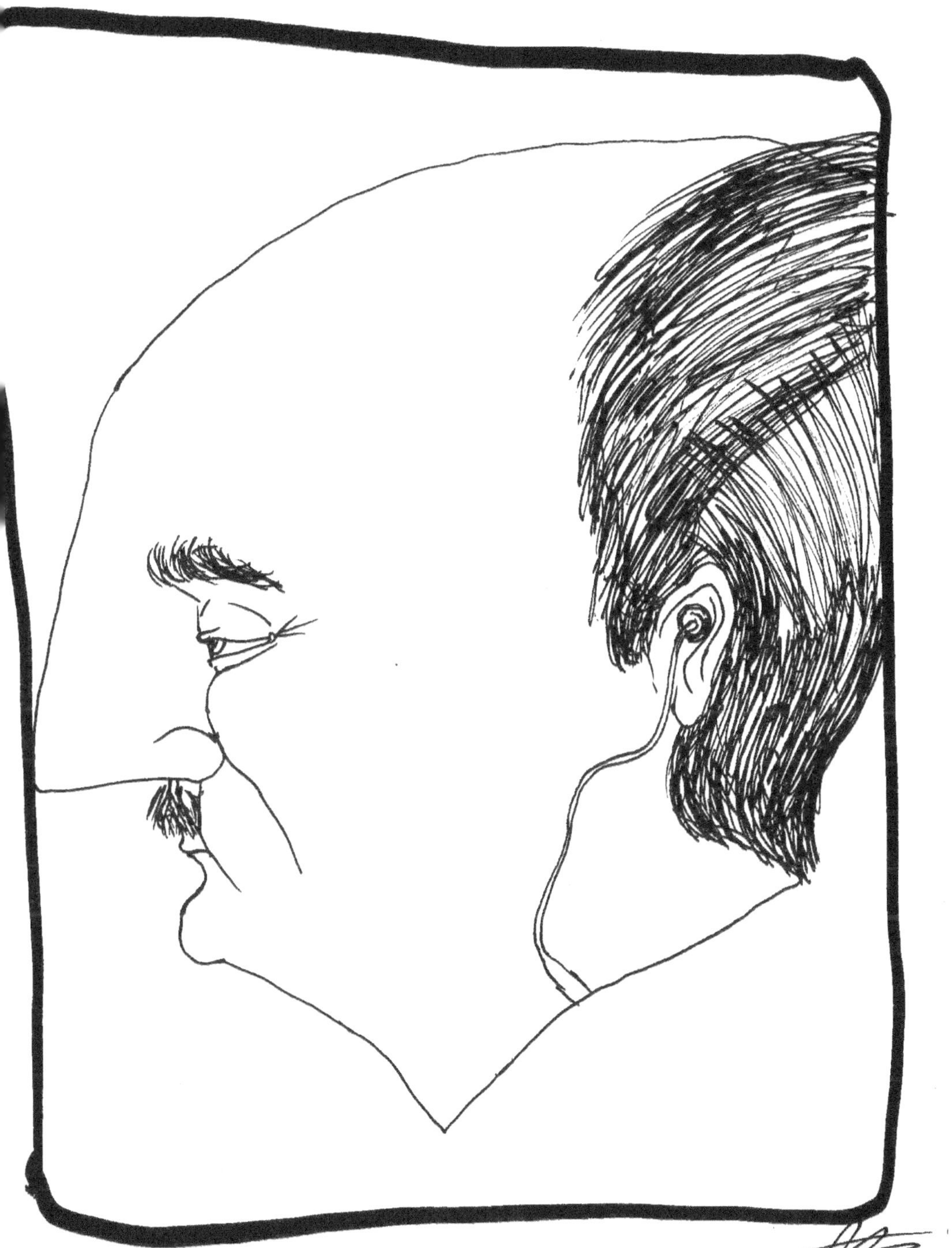

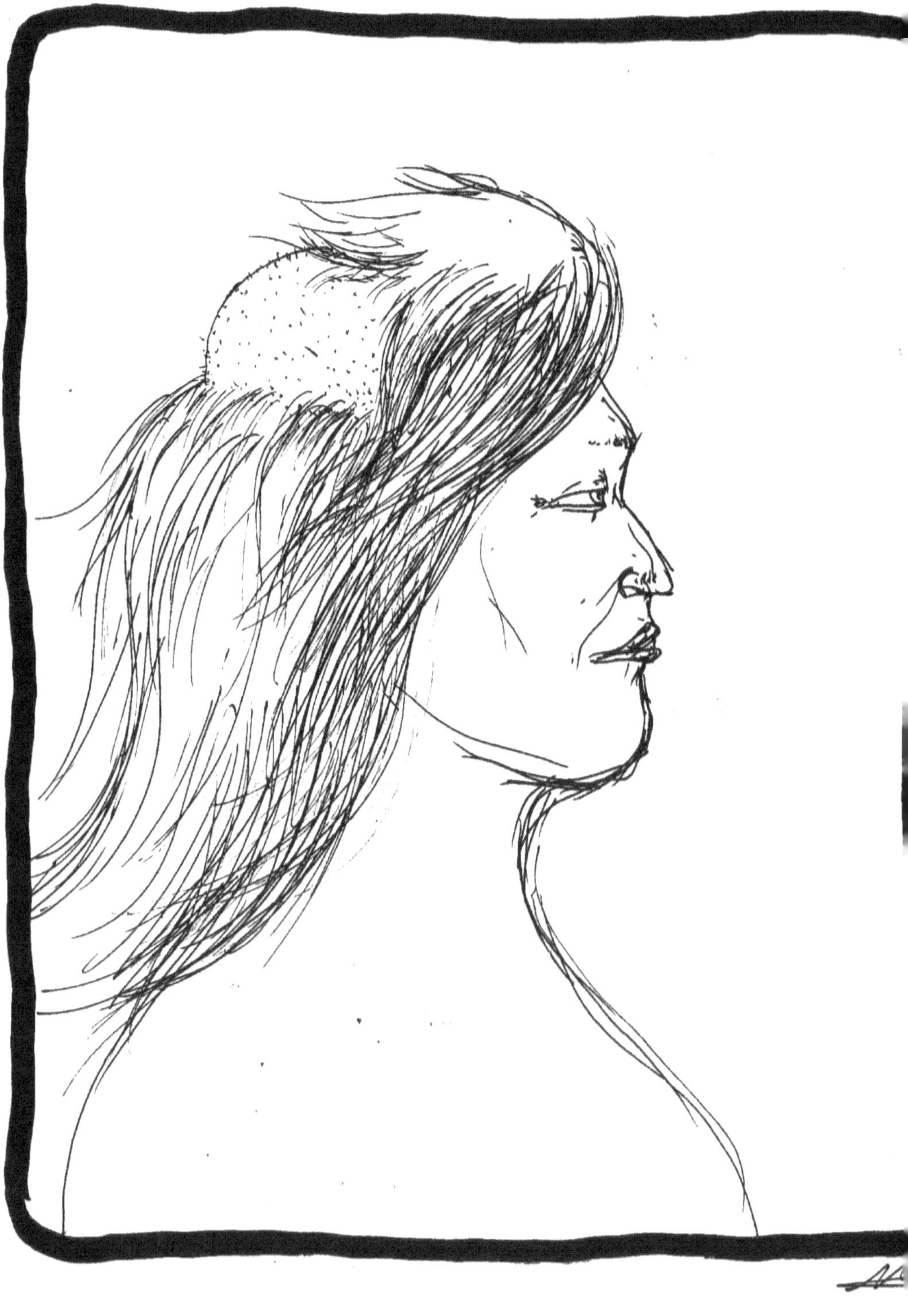

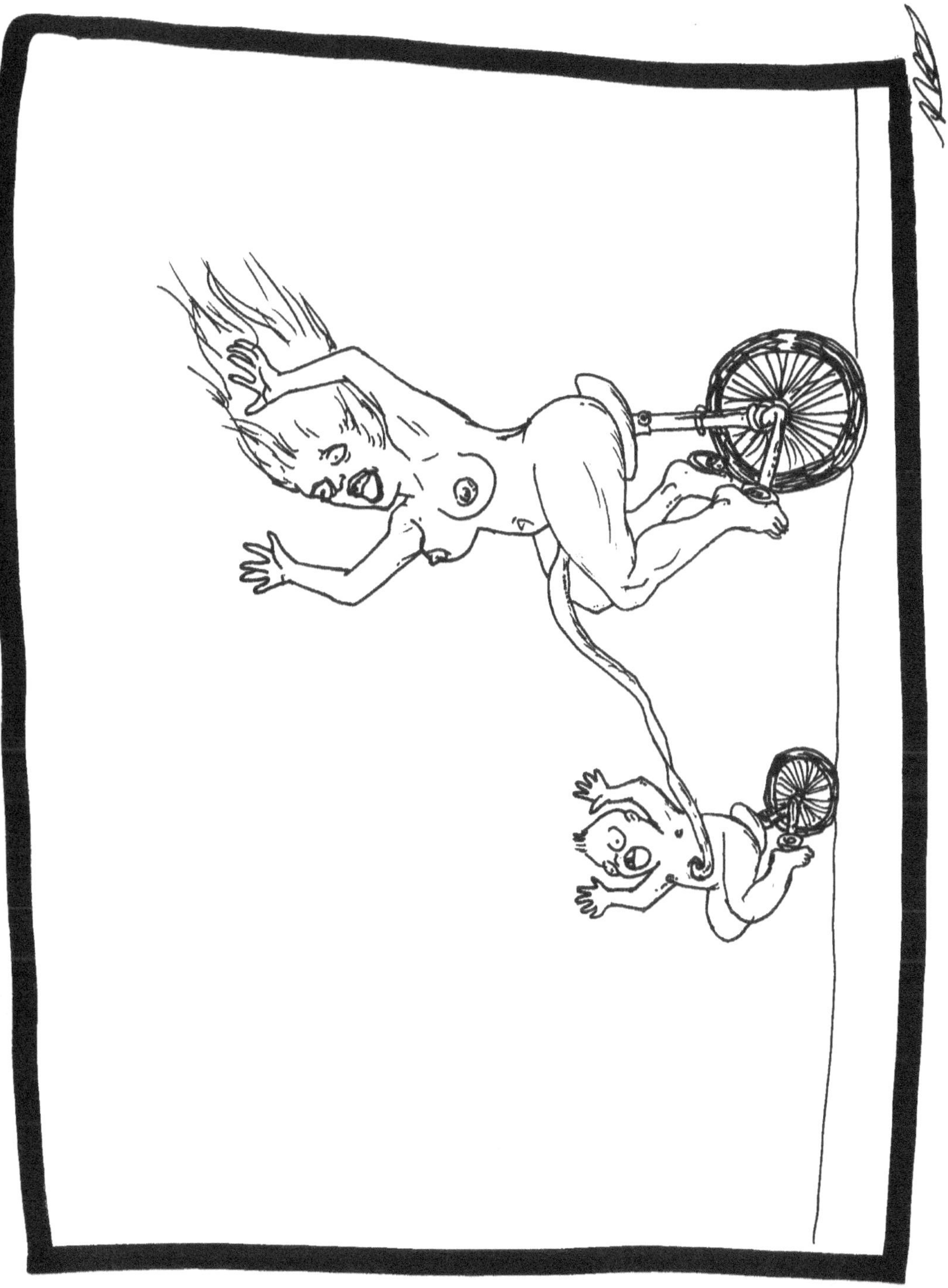

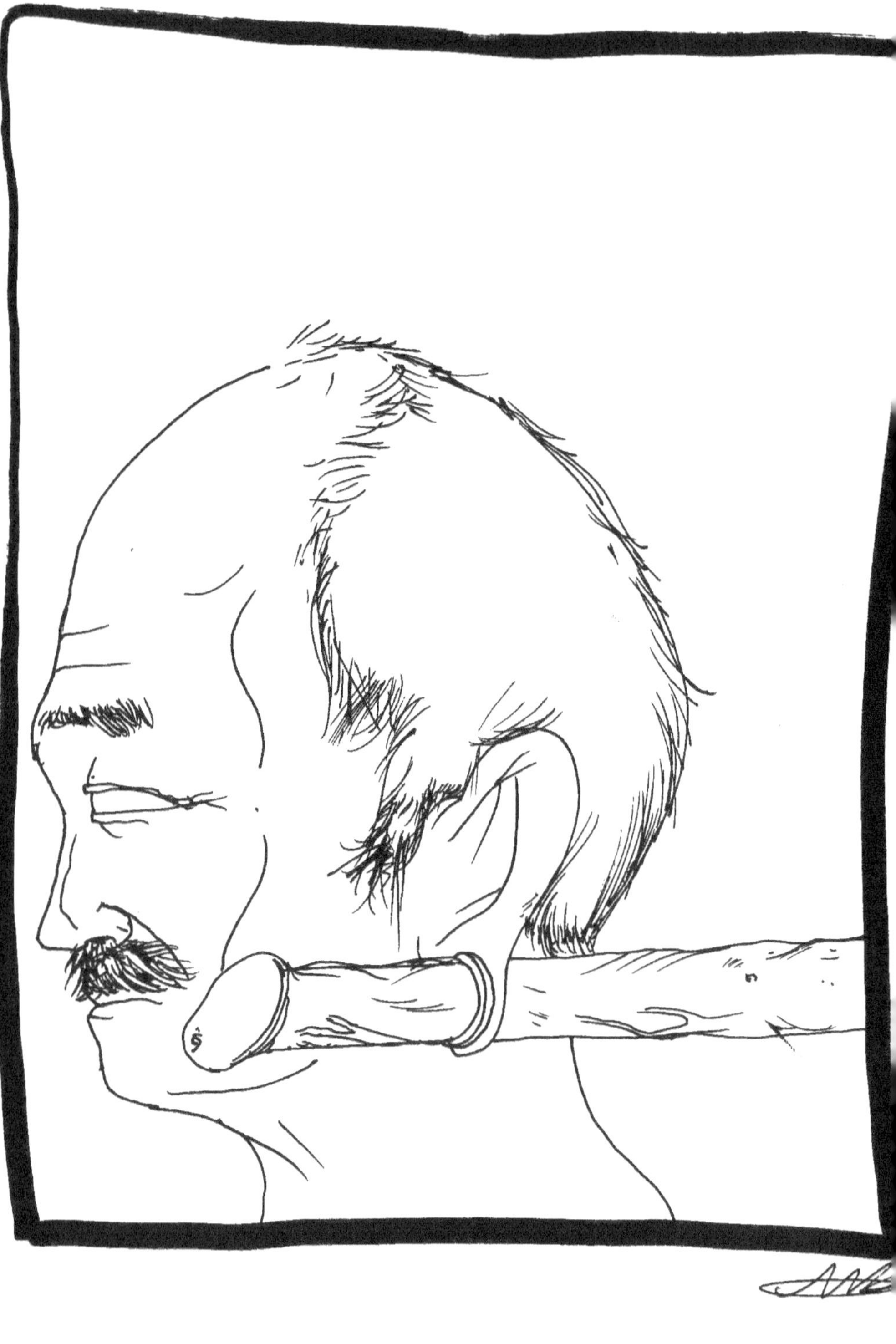

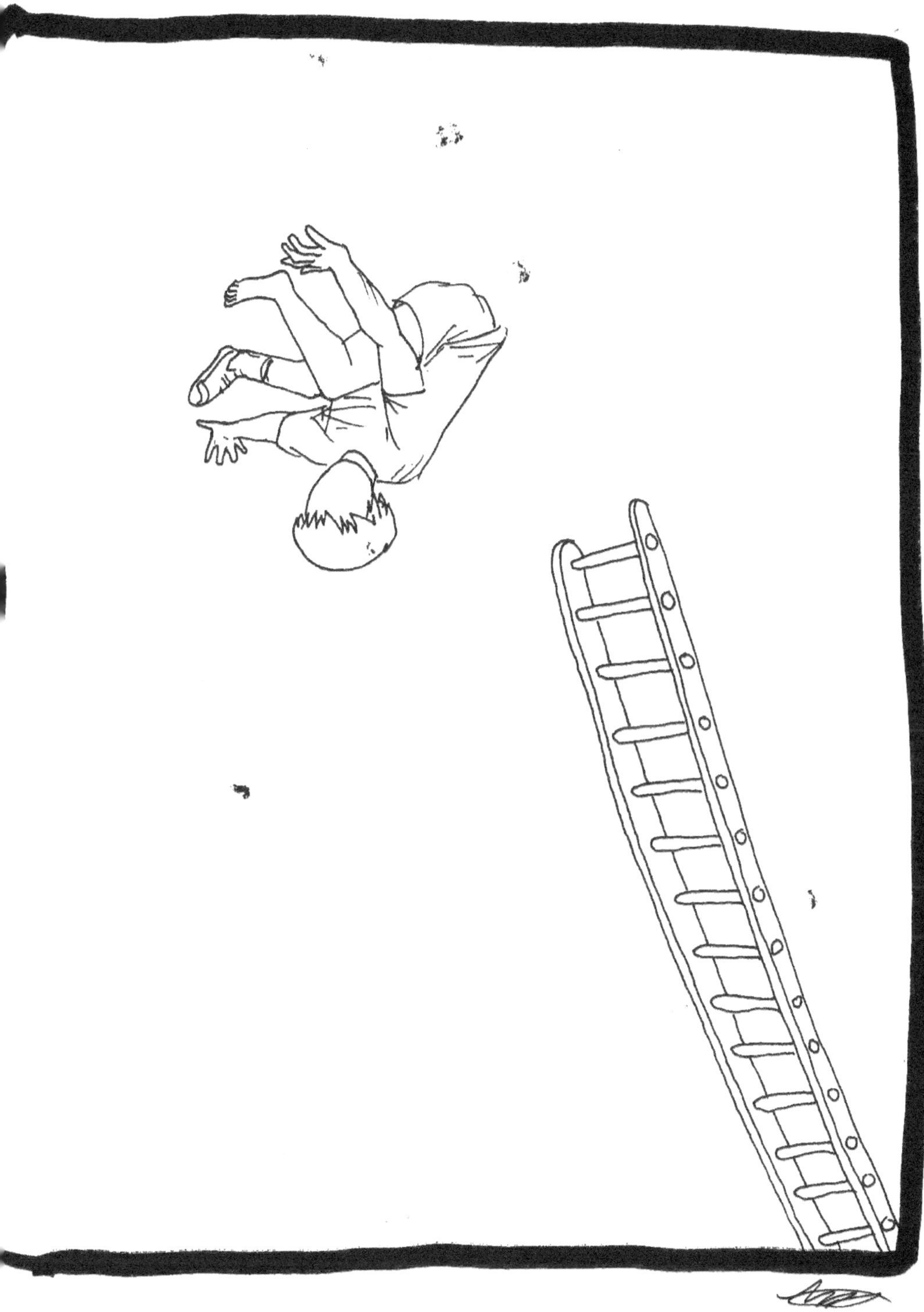

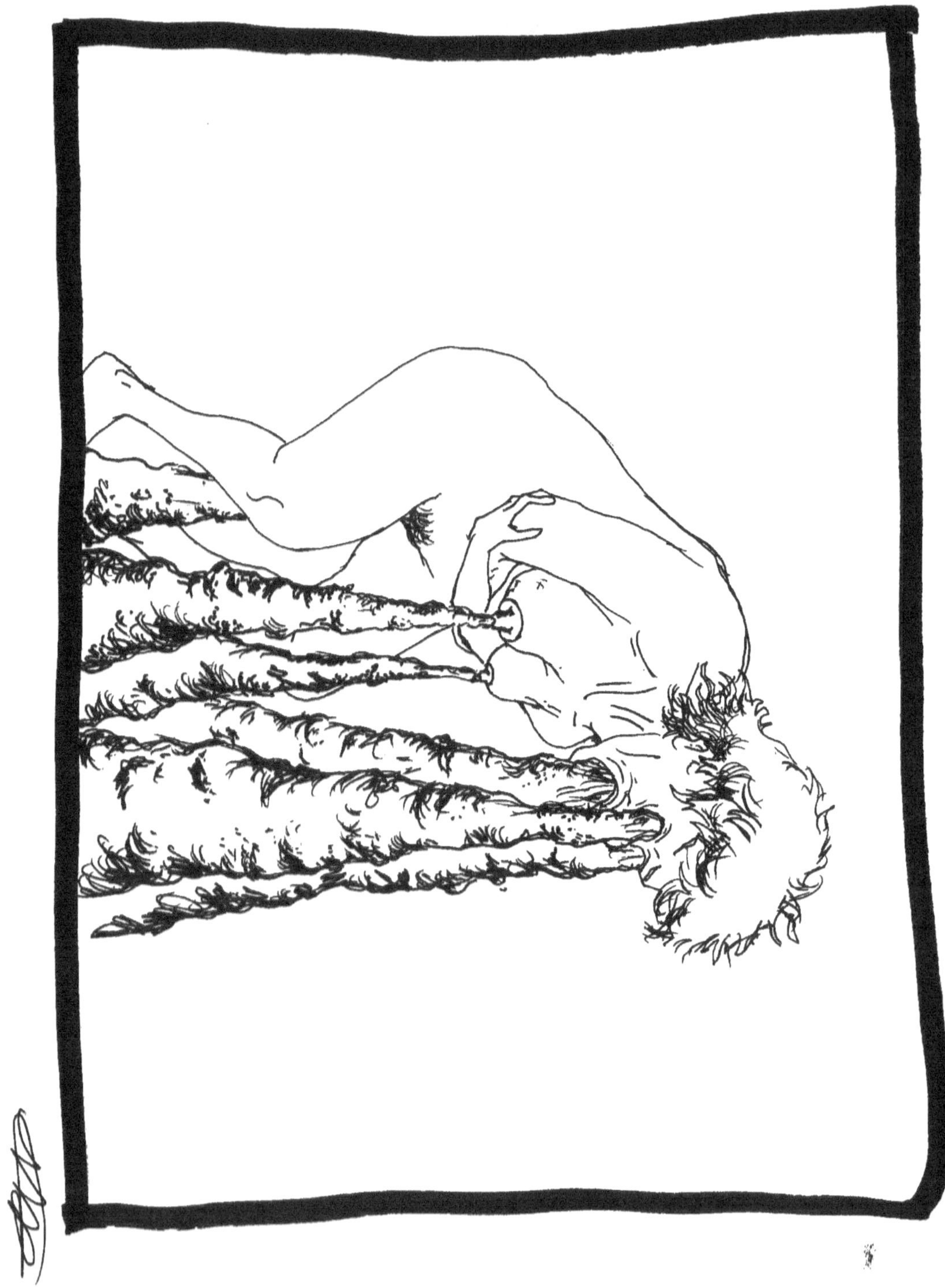

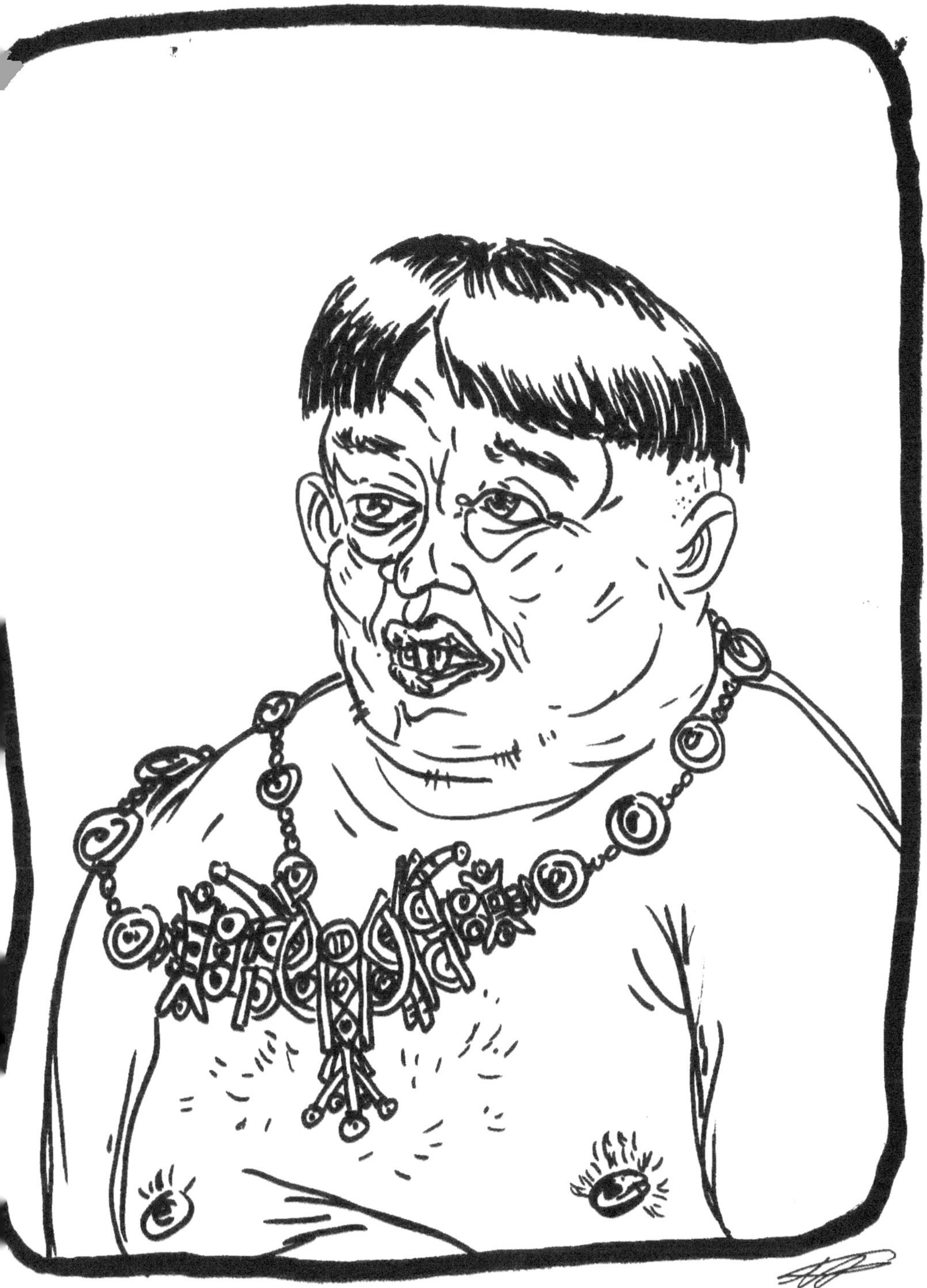

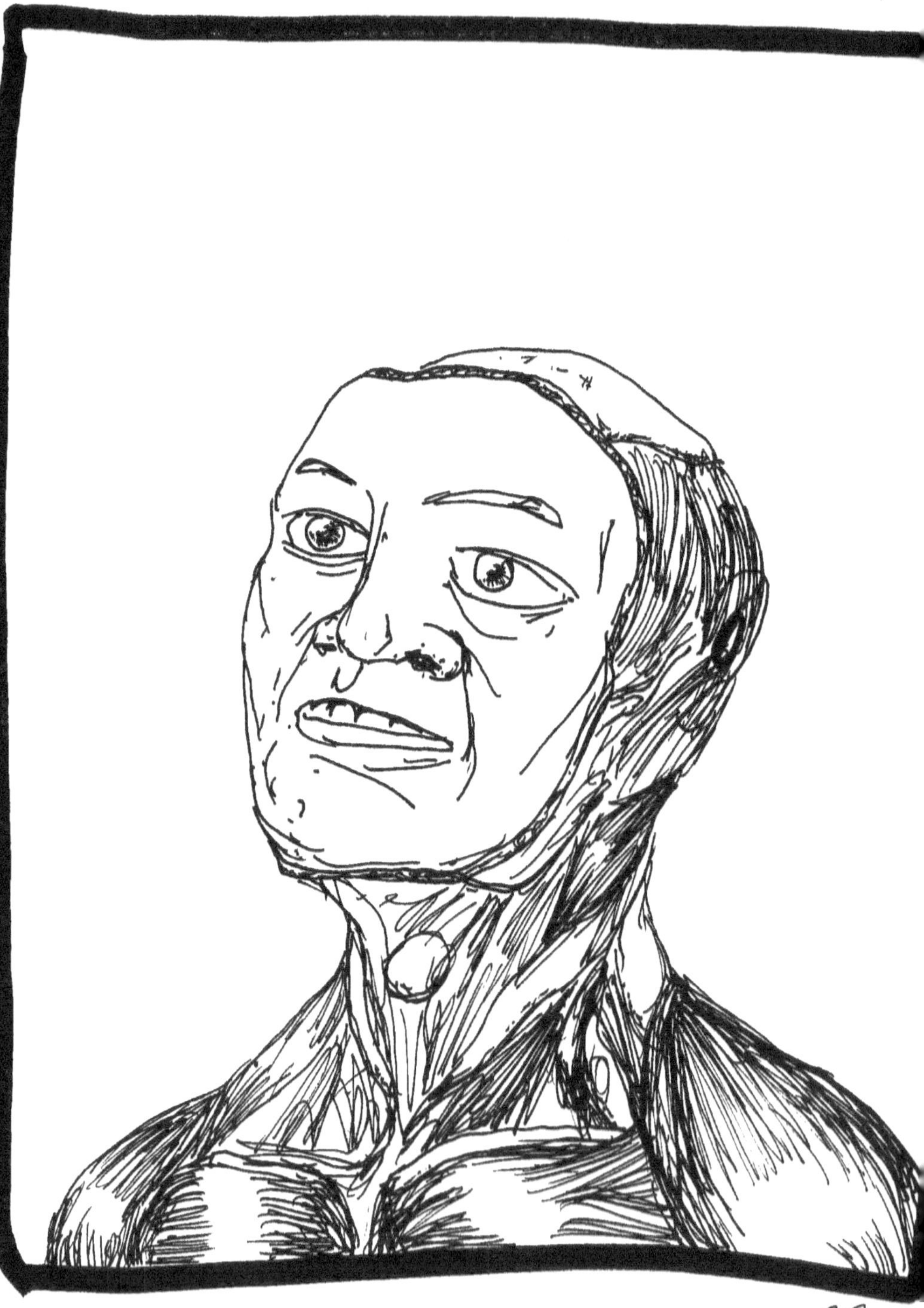

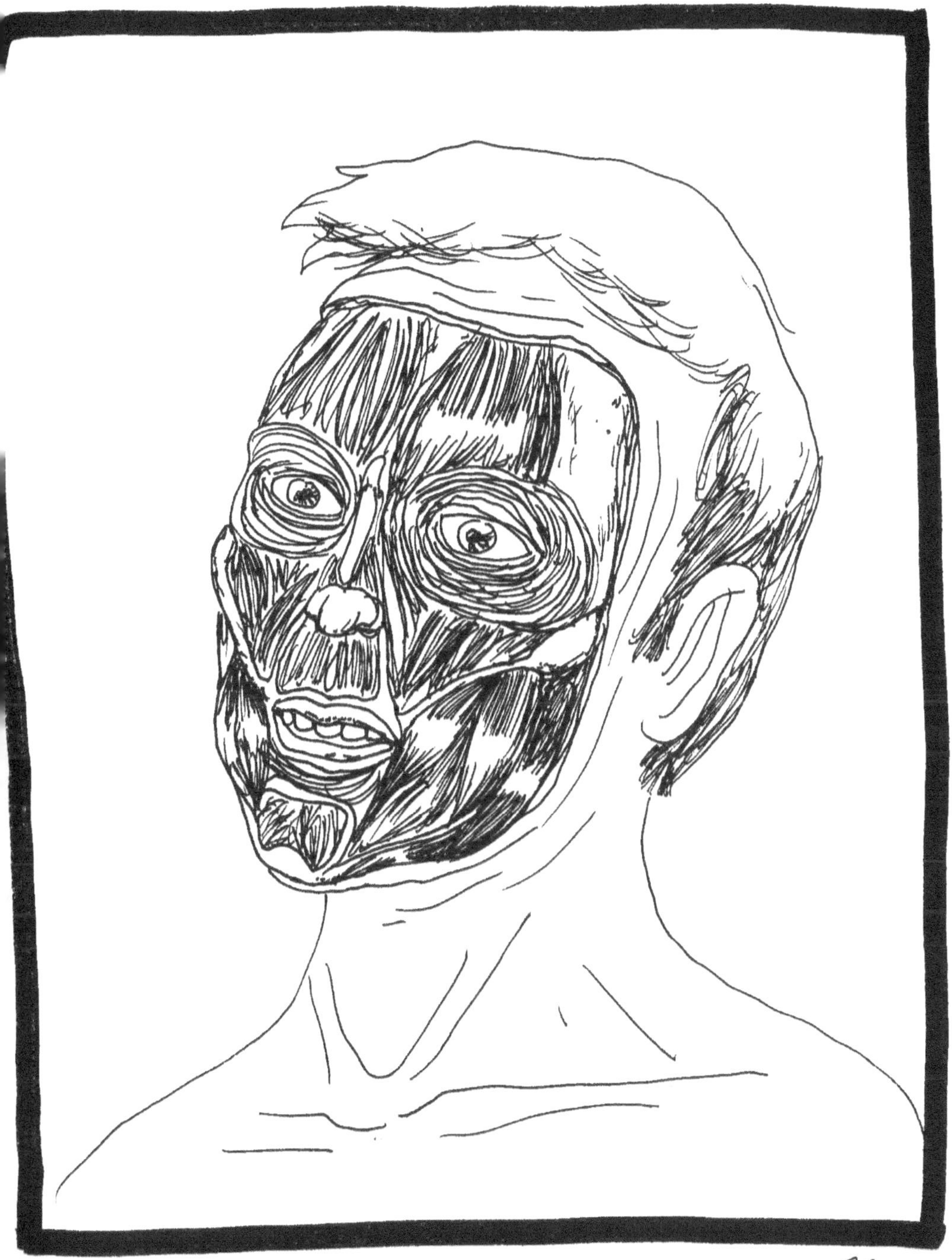

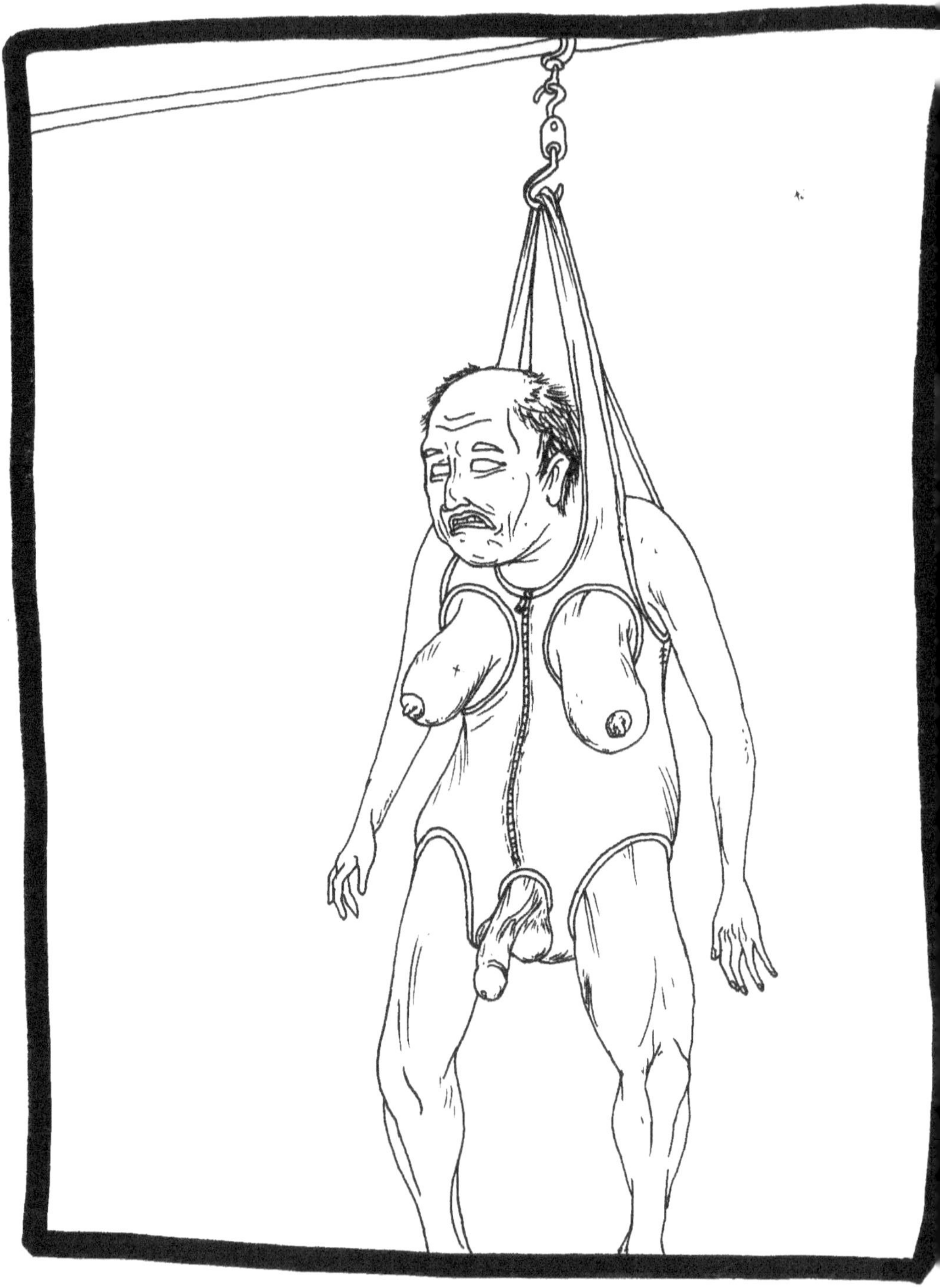

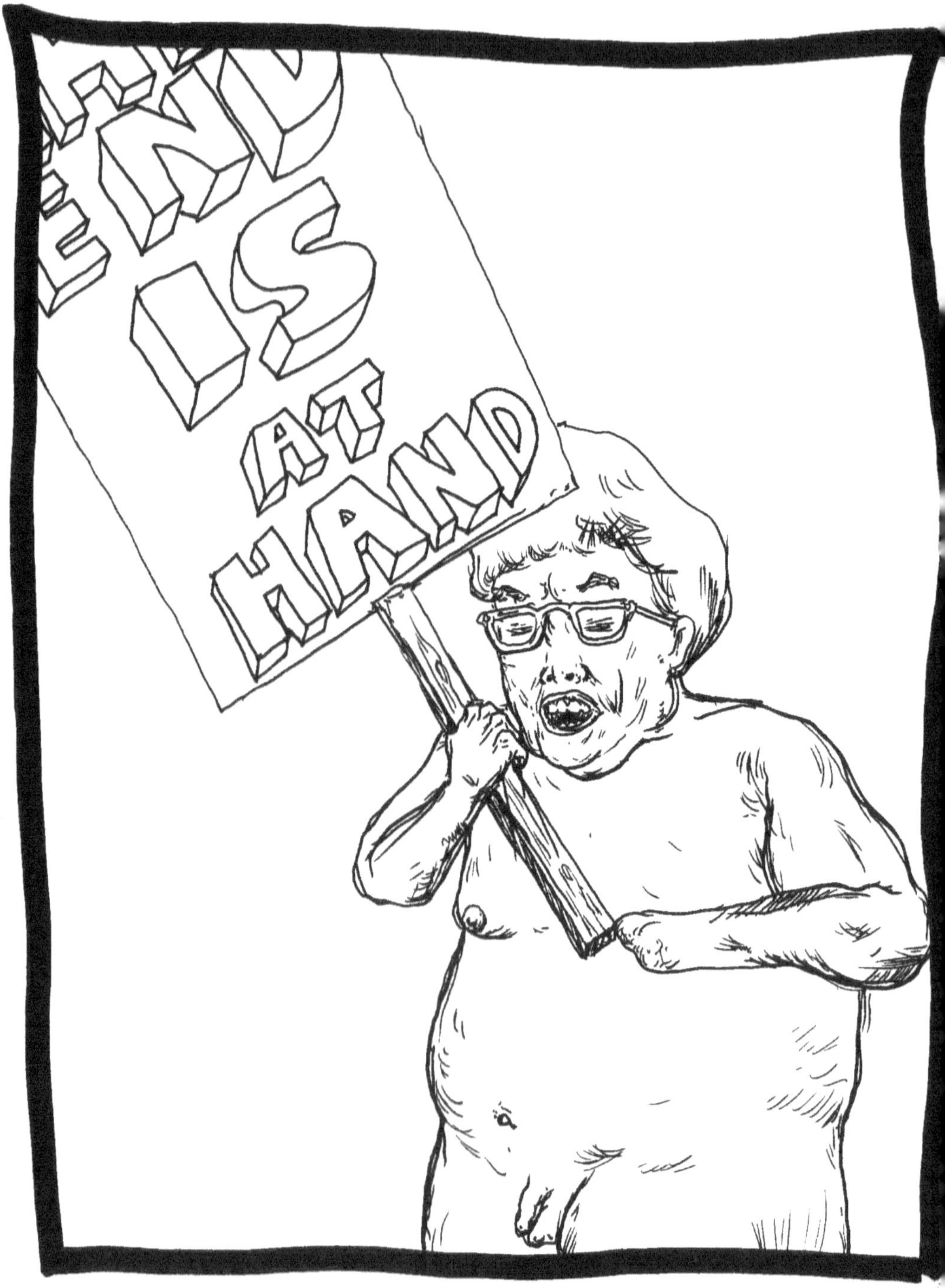
END
IS
AT
HAND

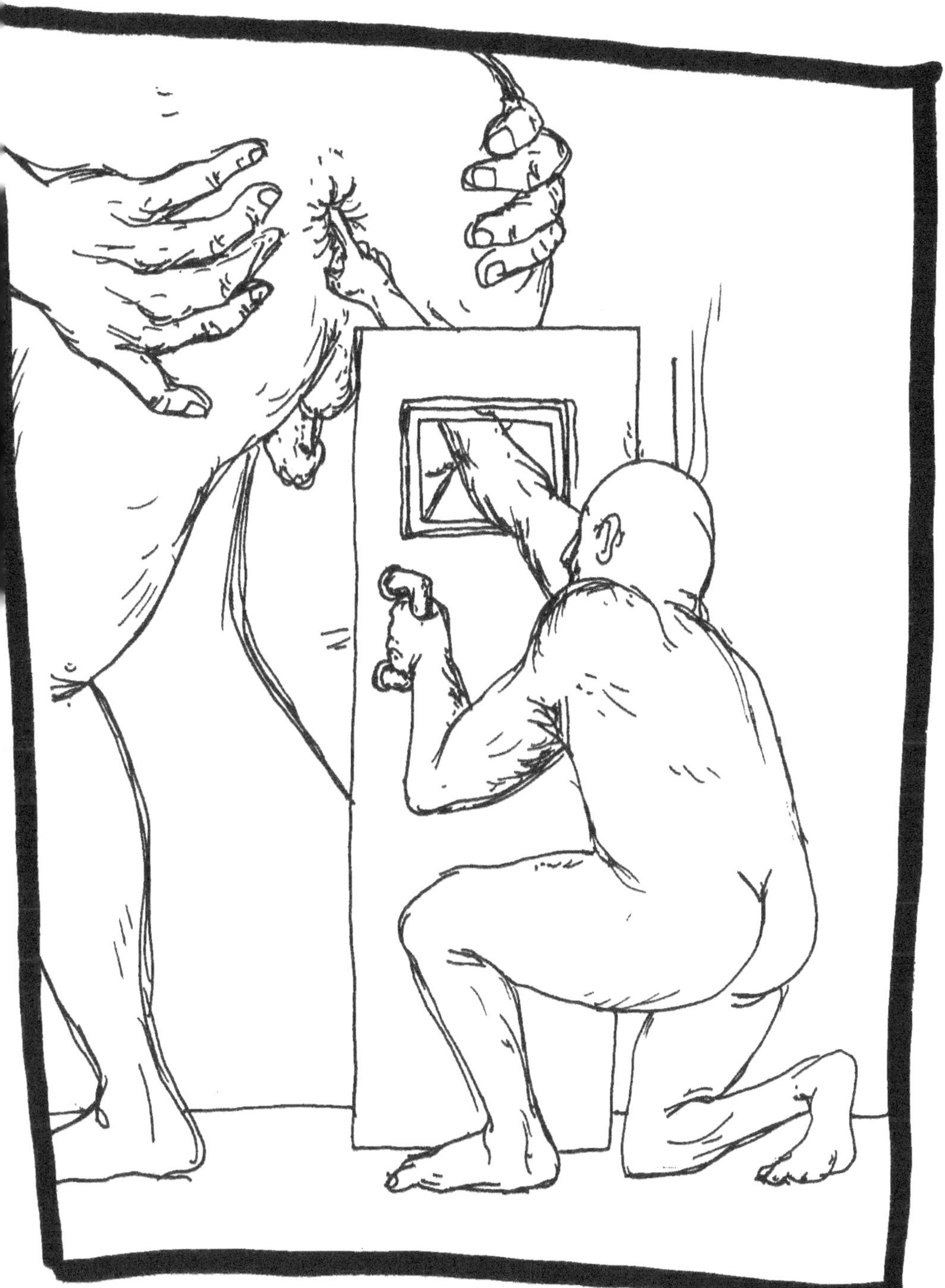

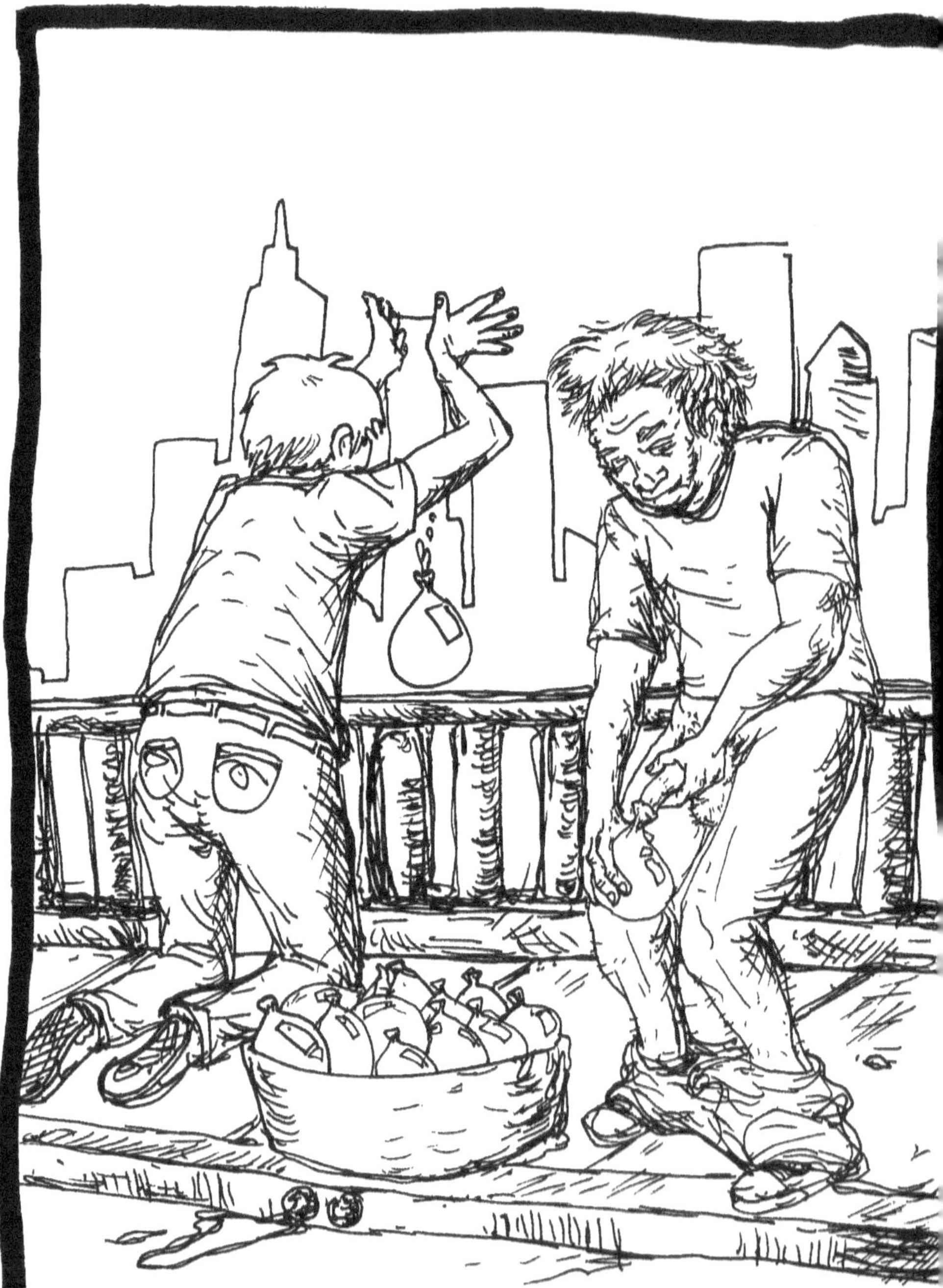

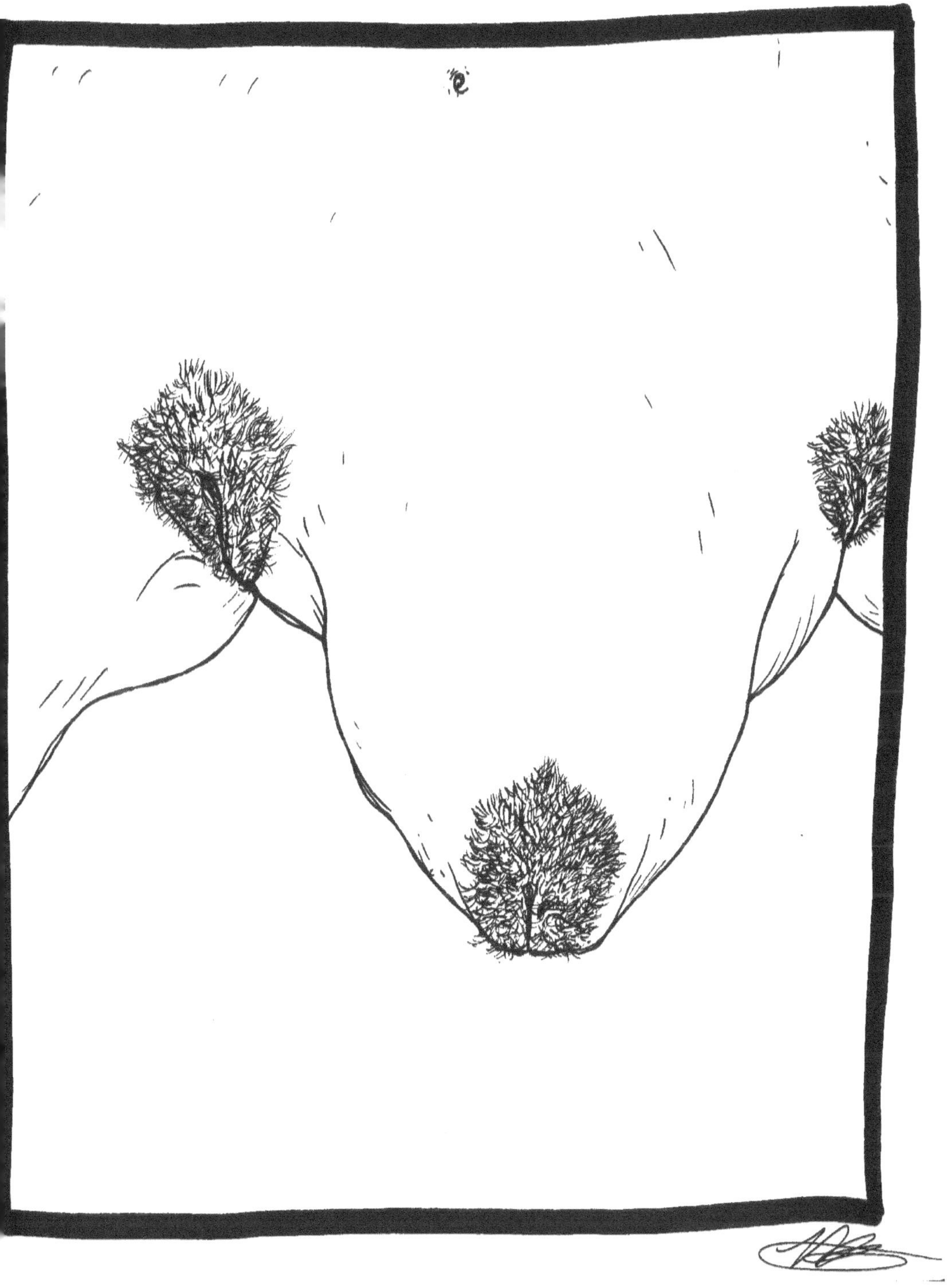

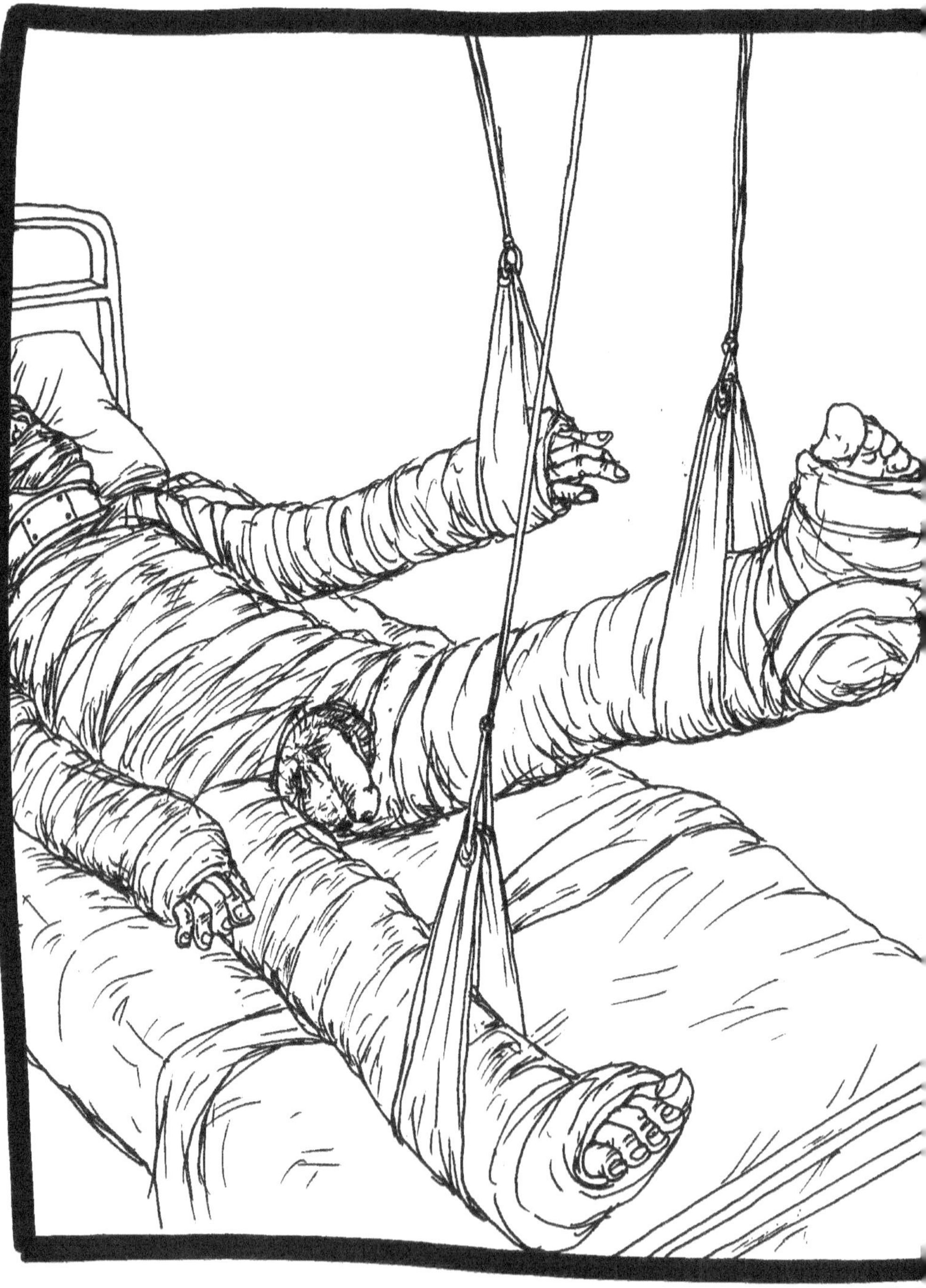

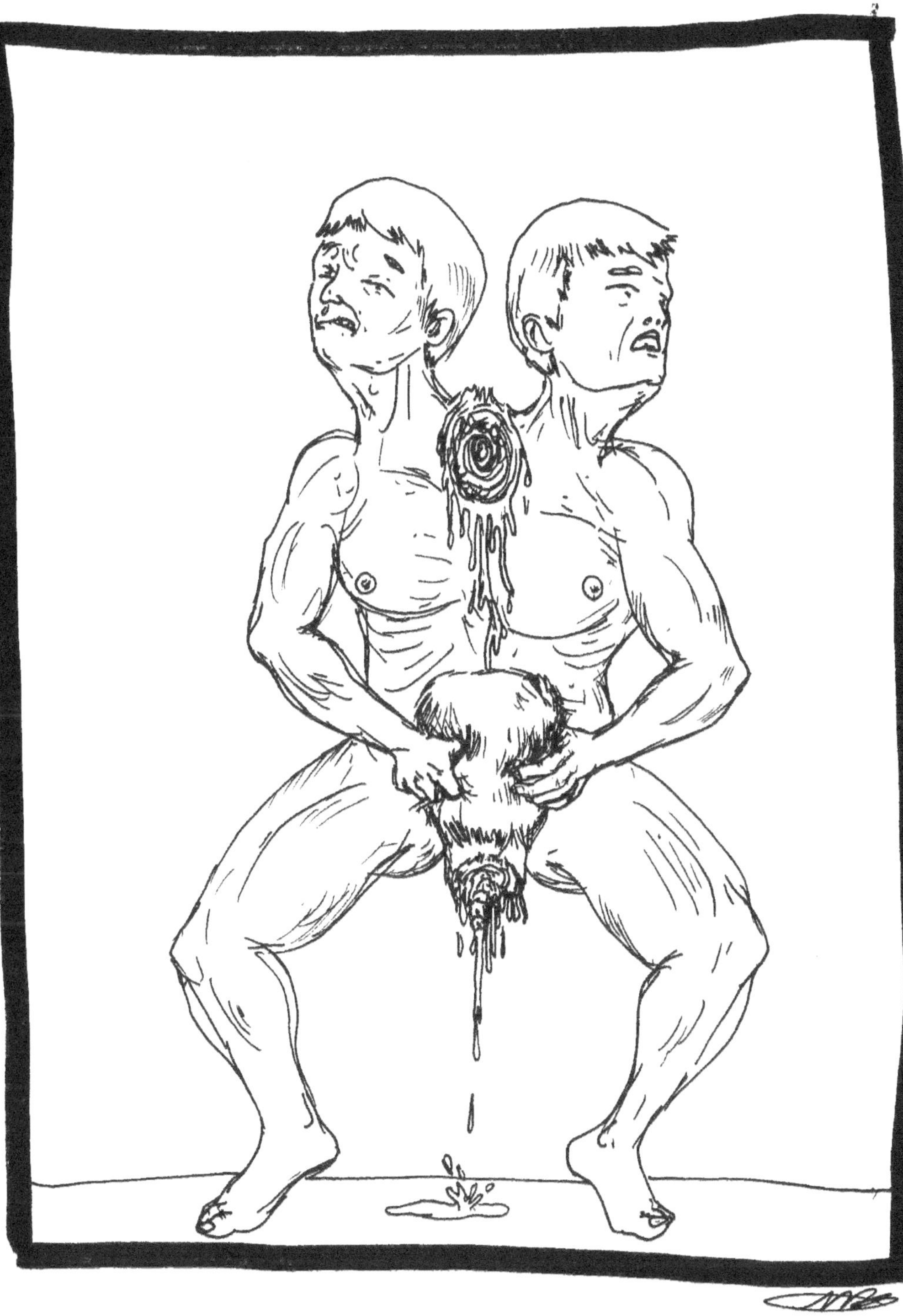

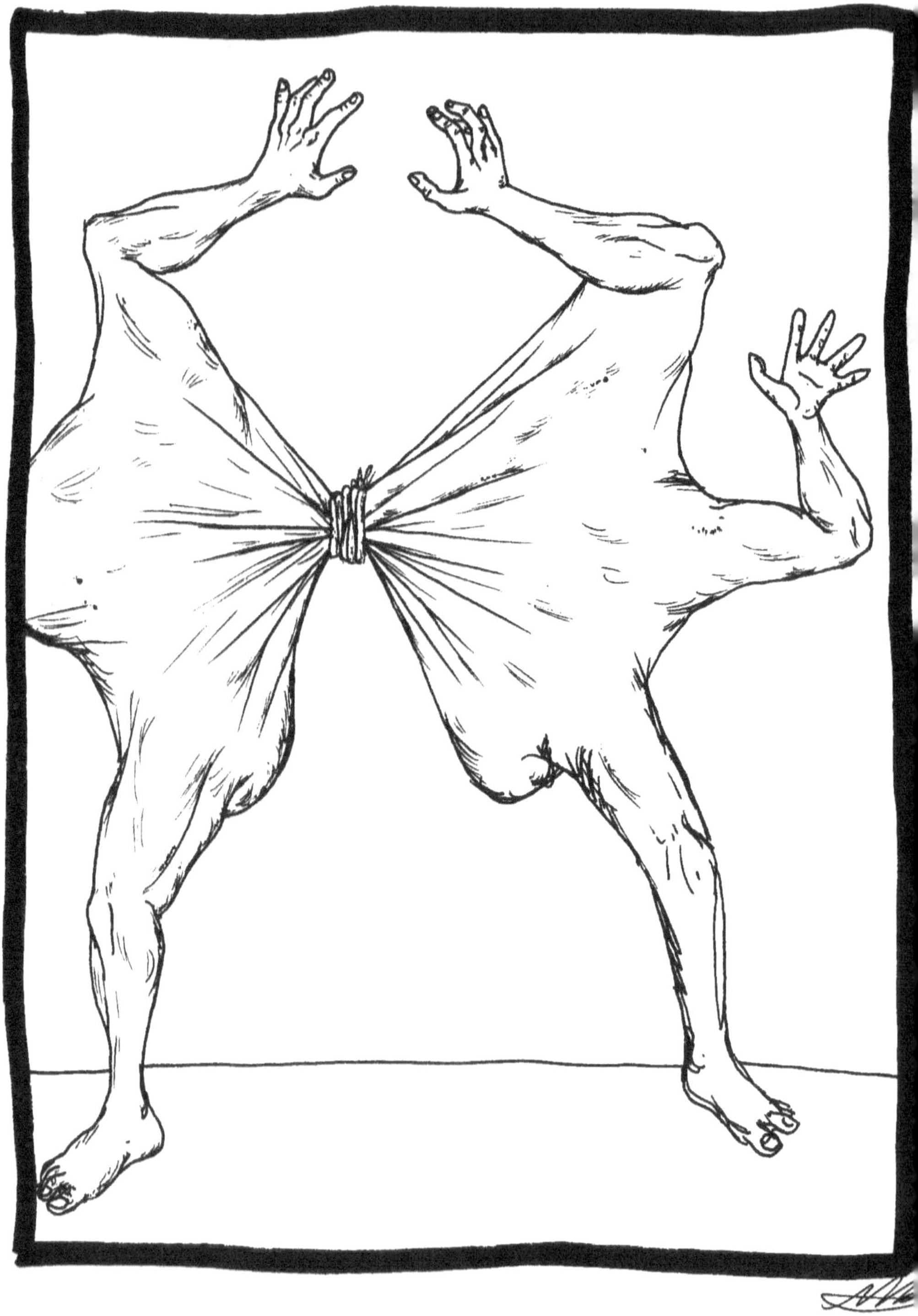

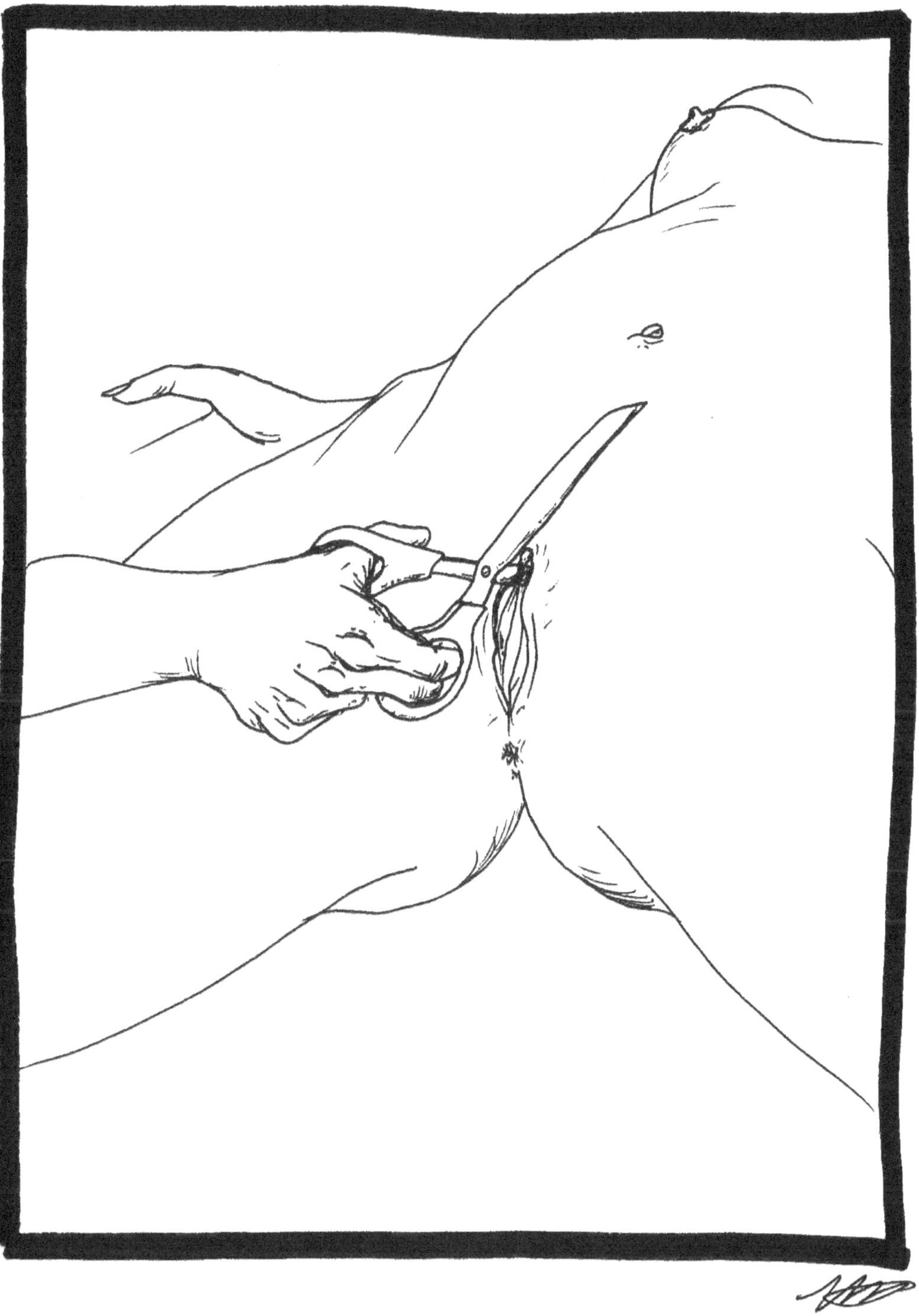

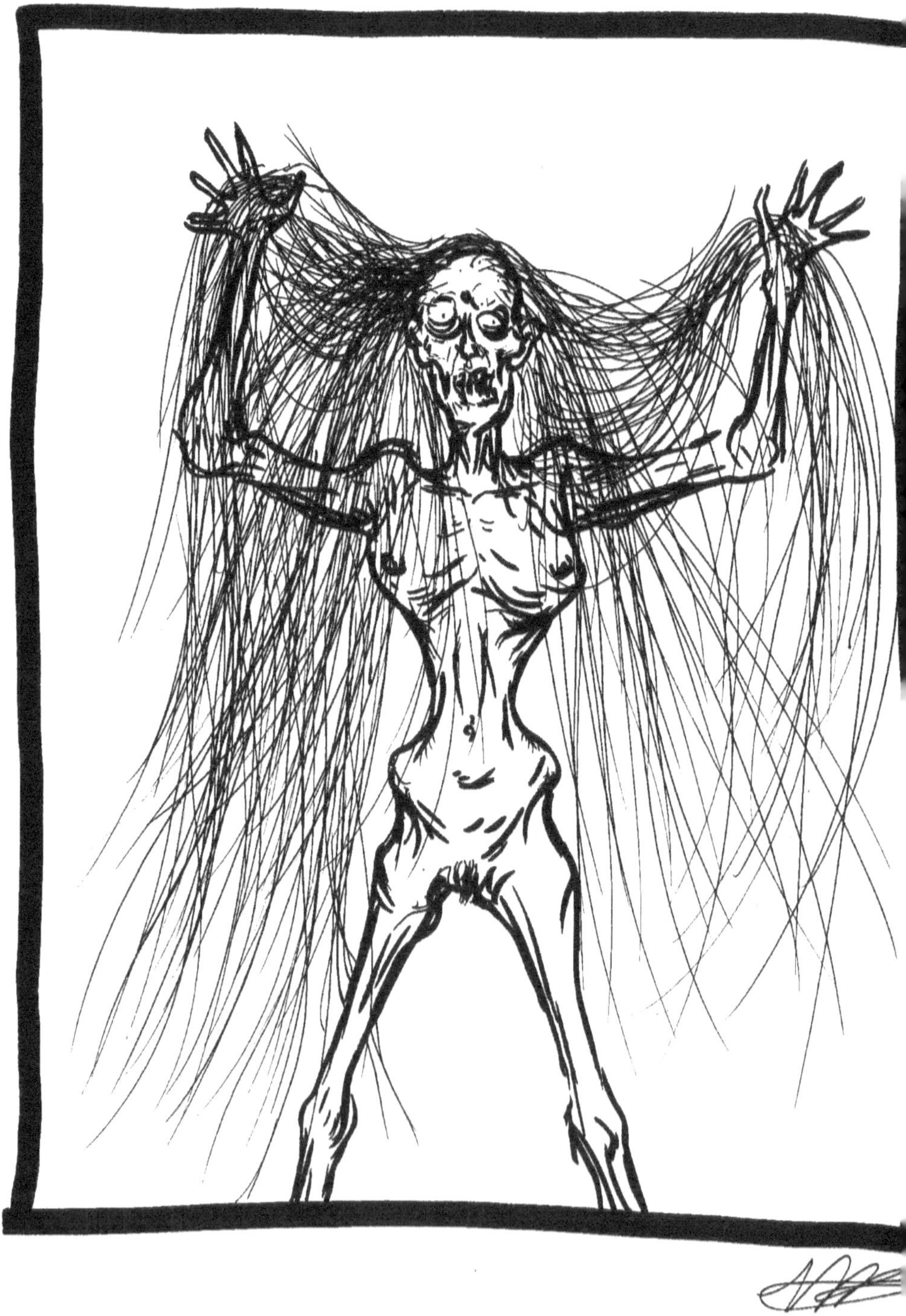

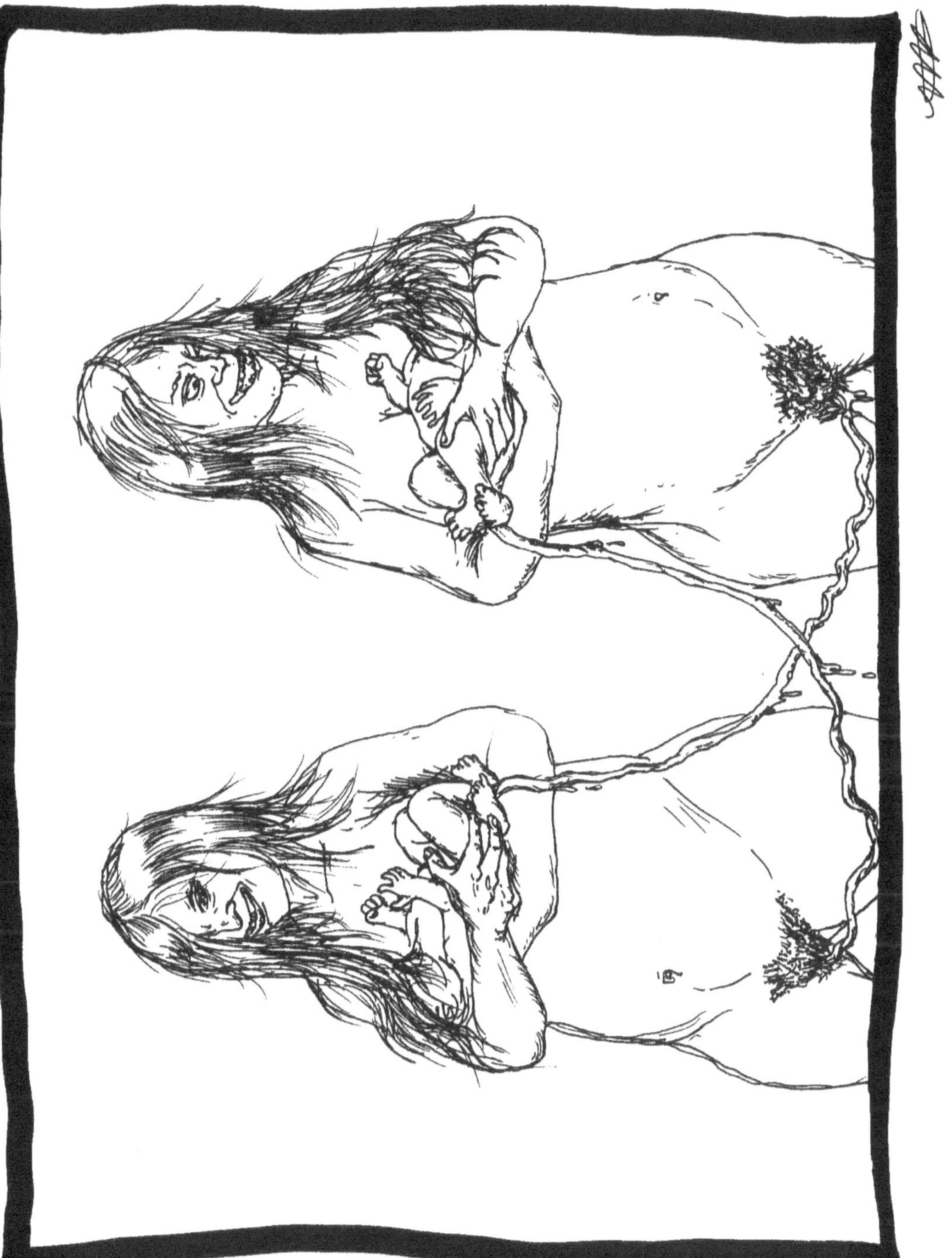

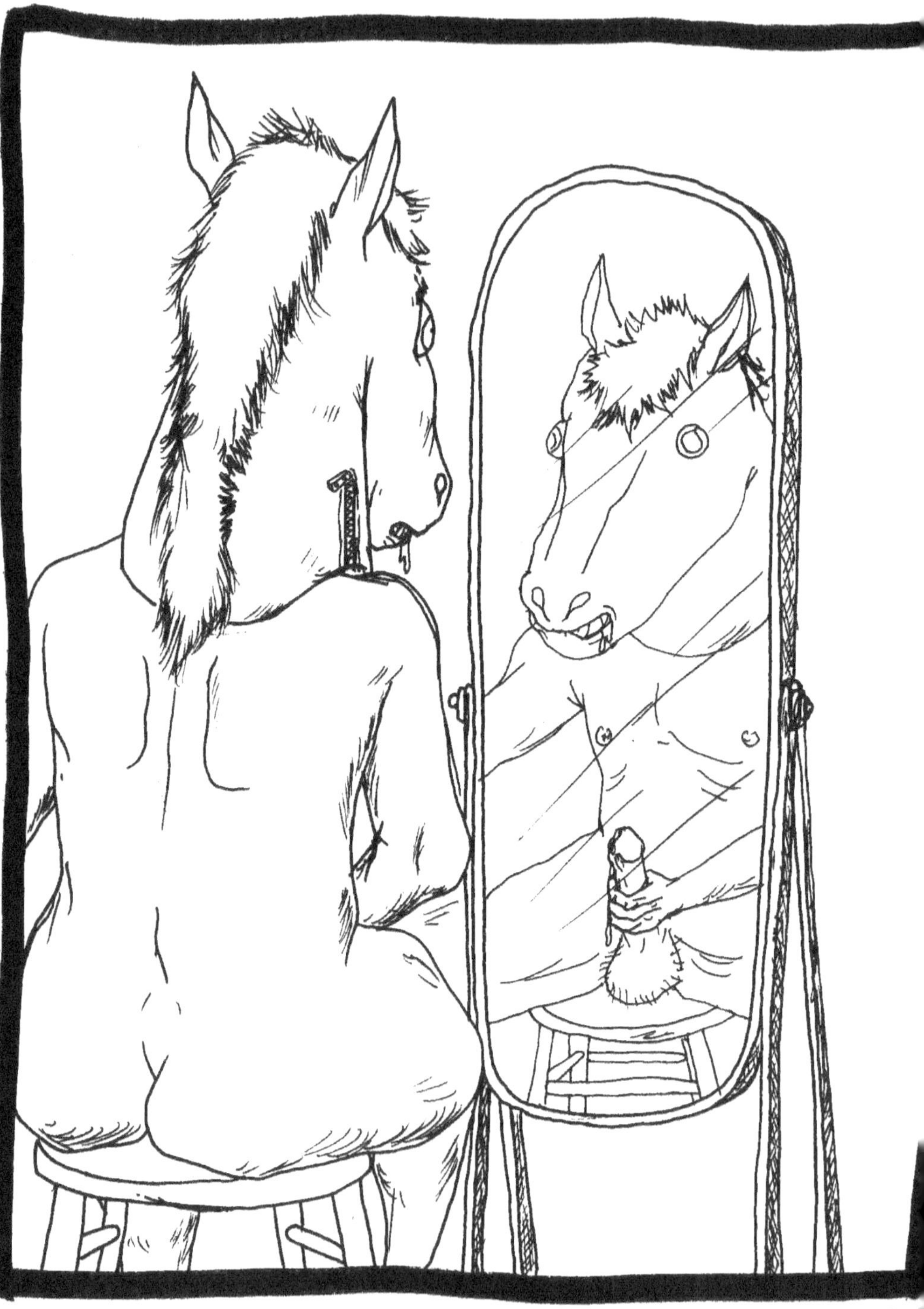

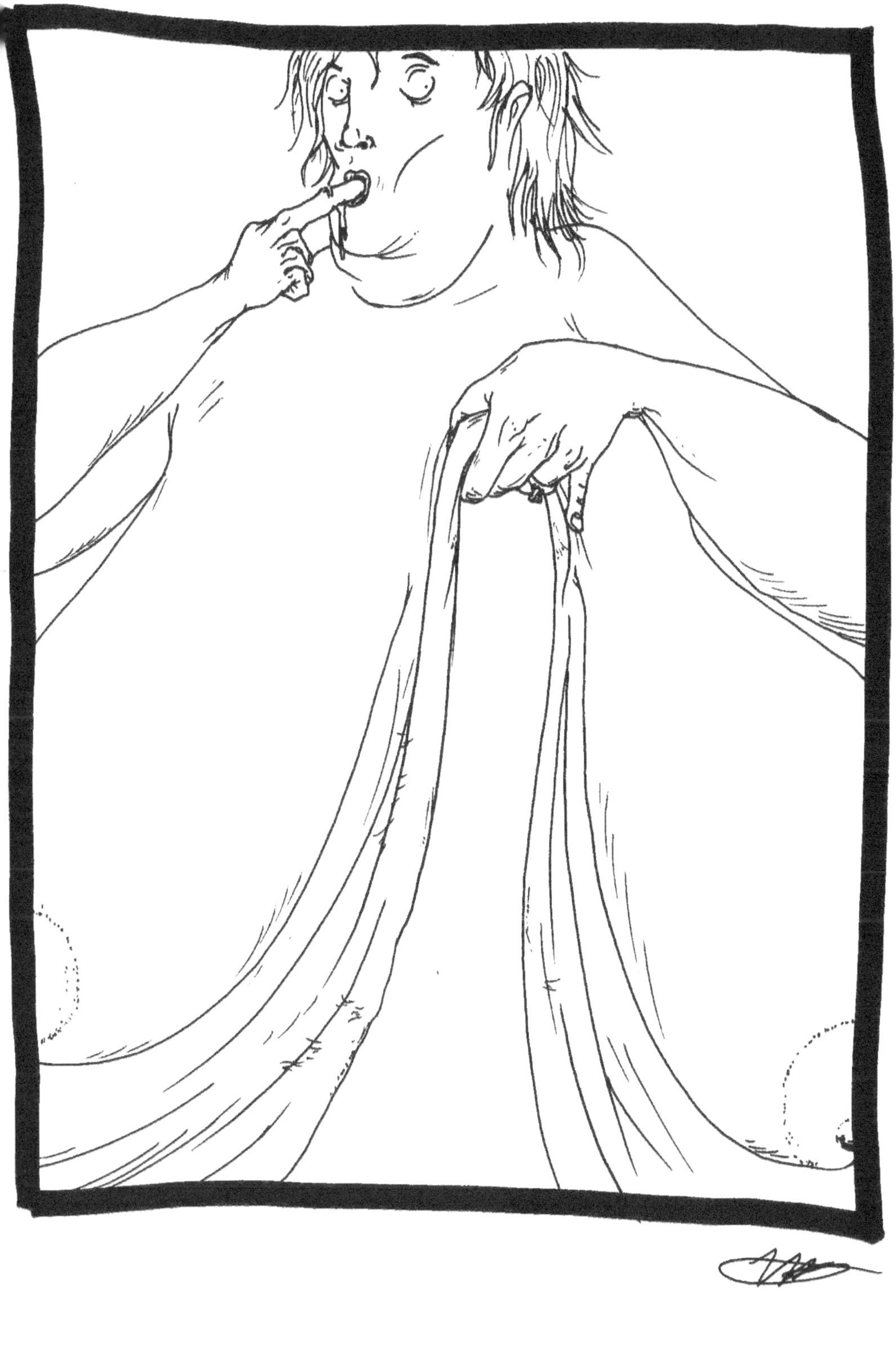

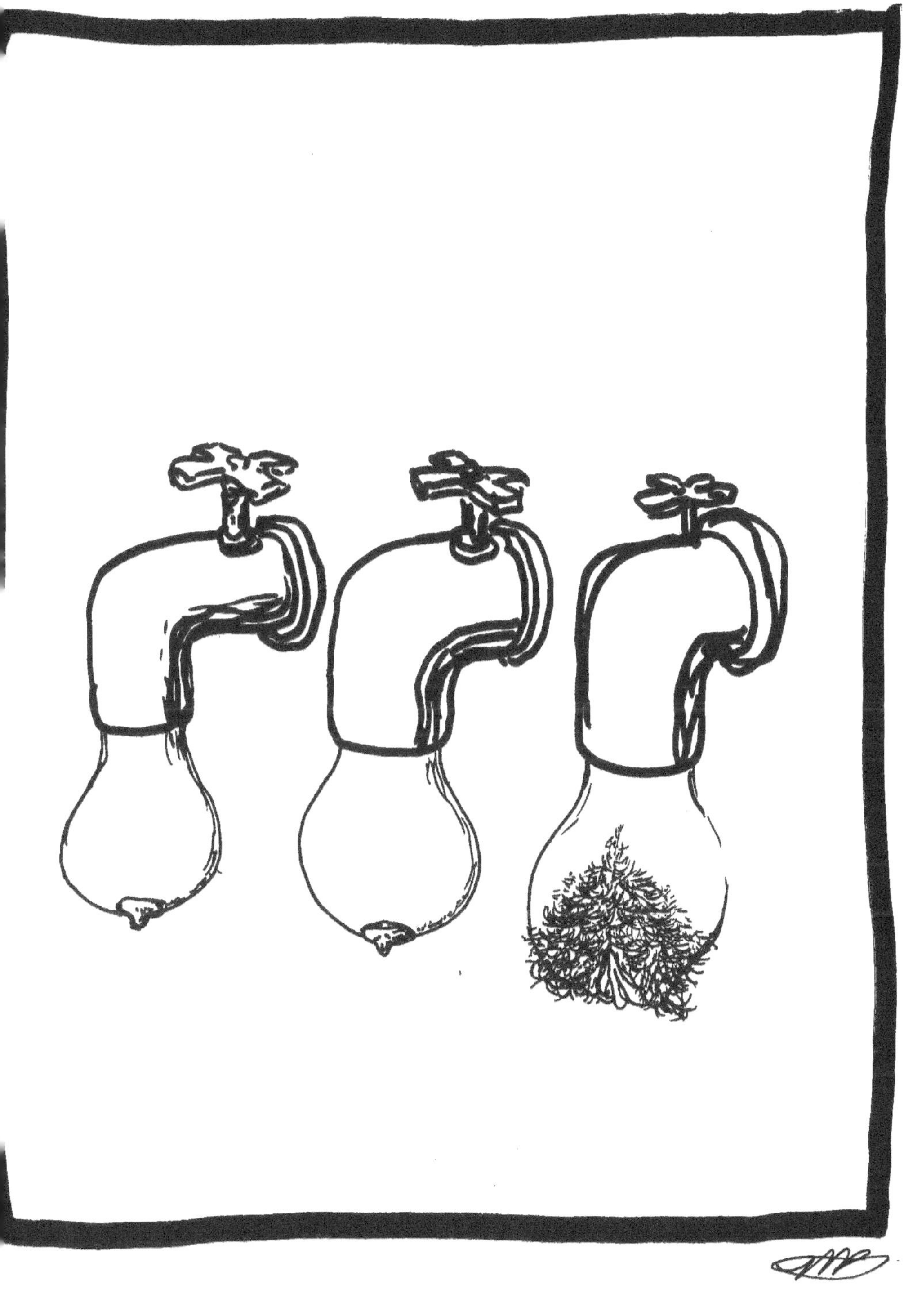

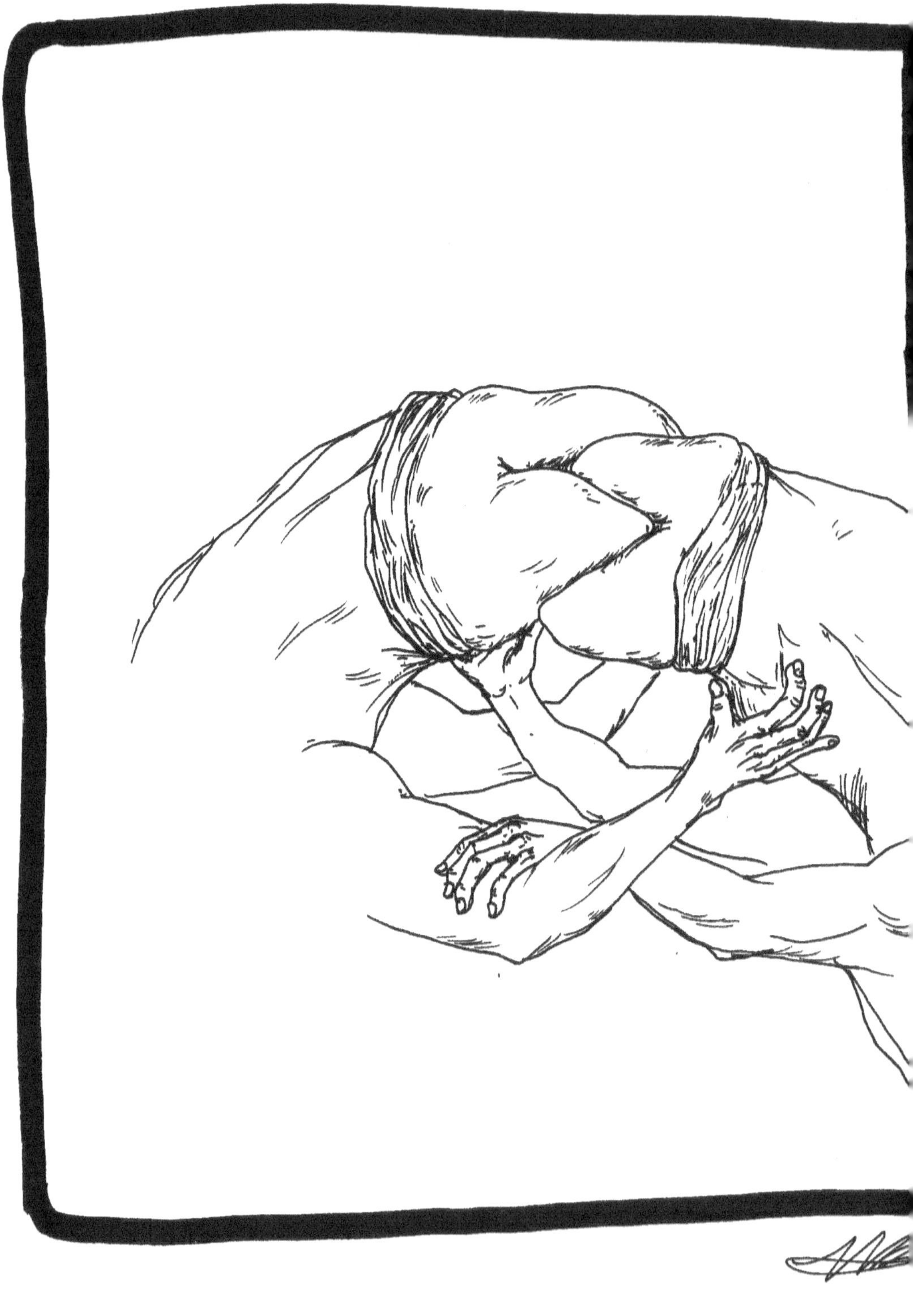

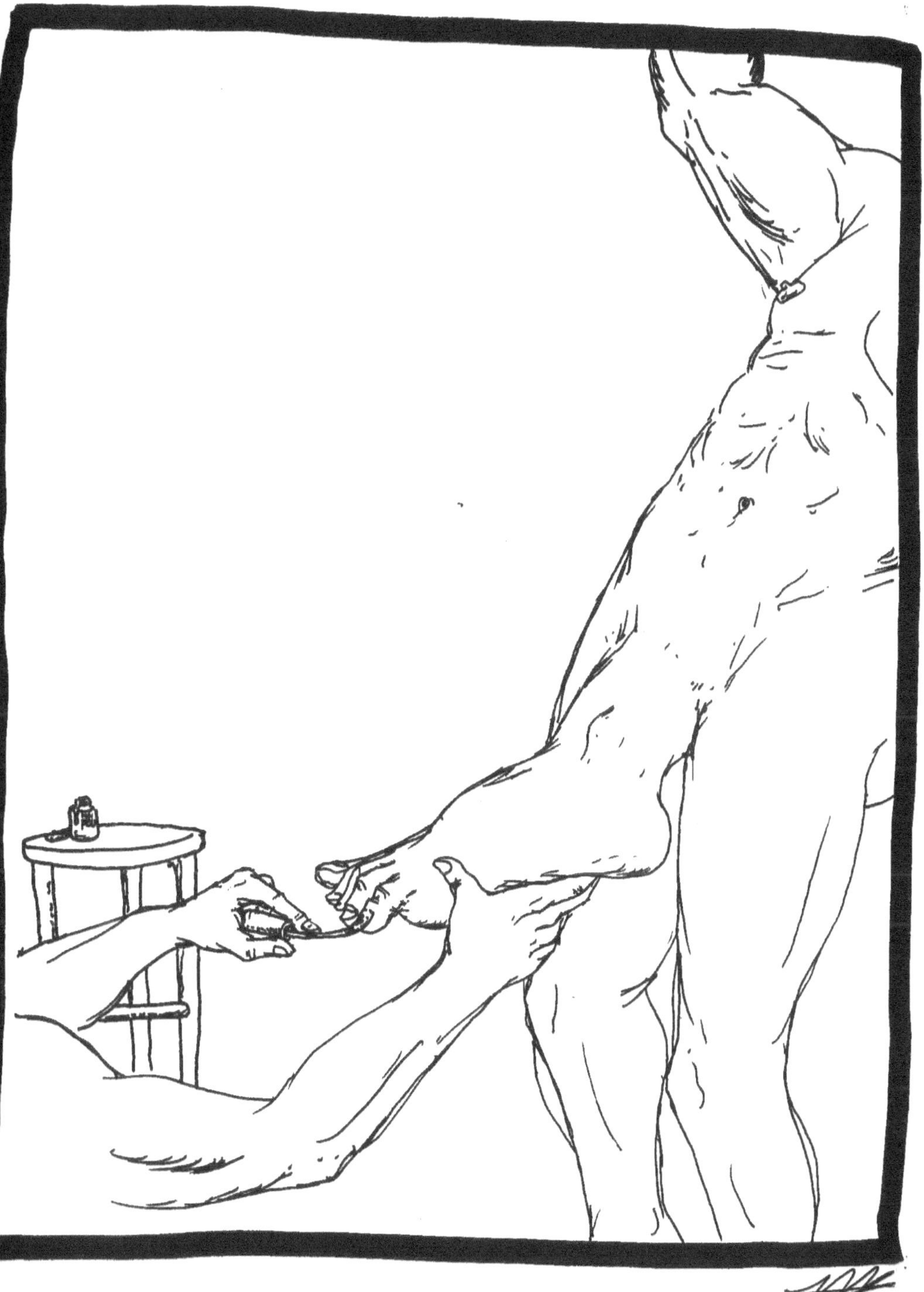

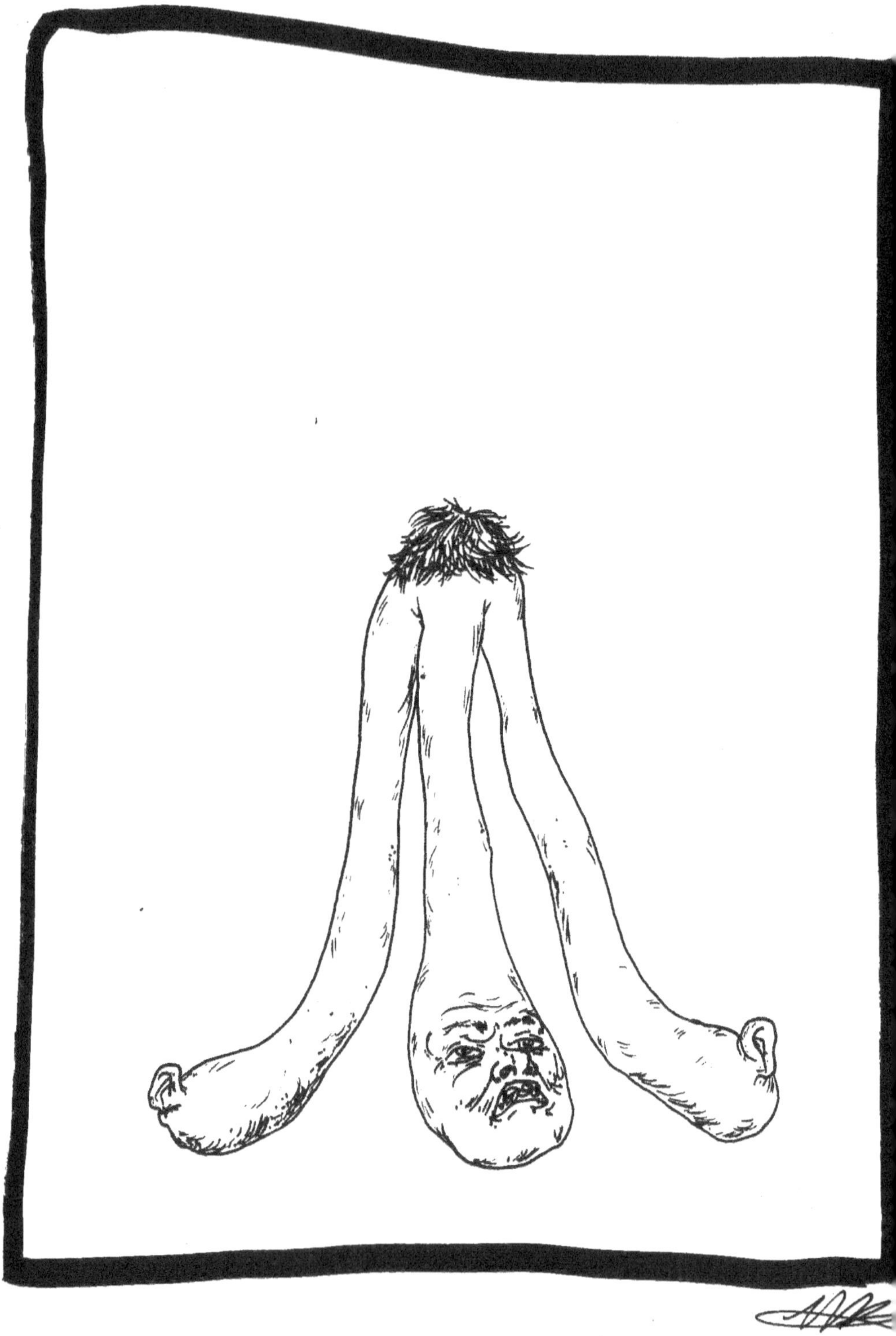

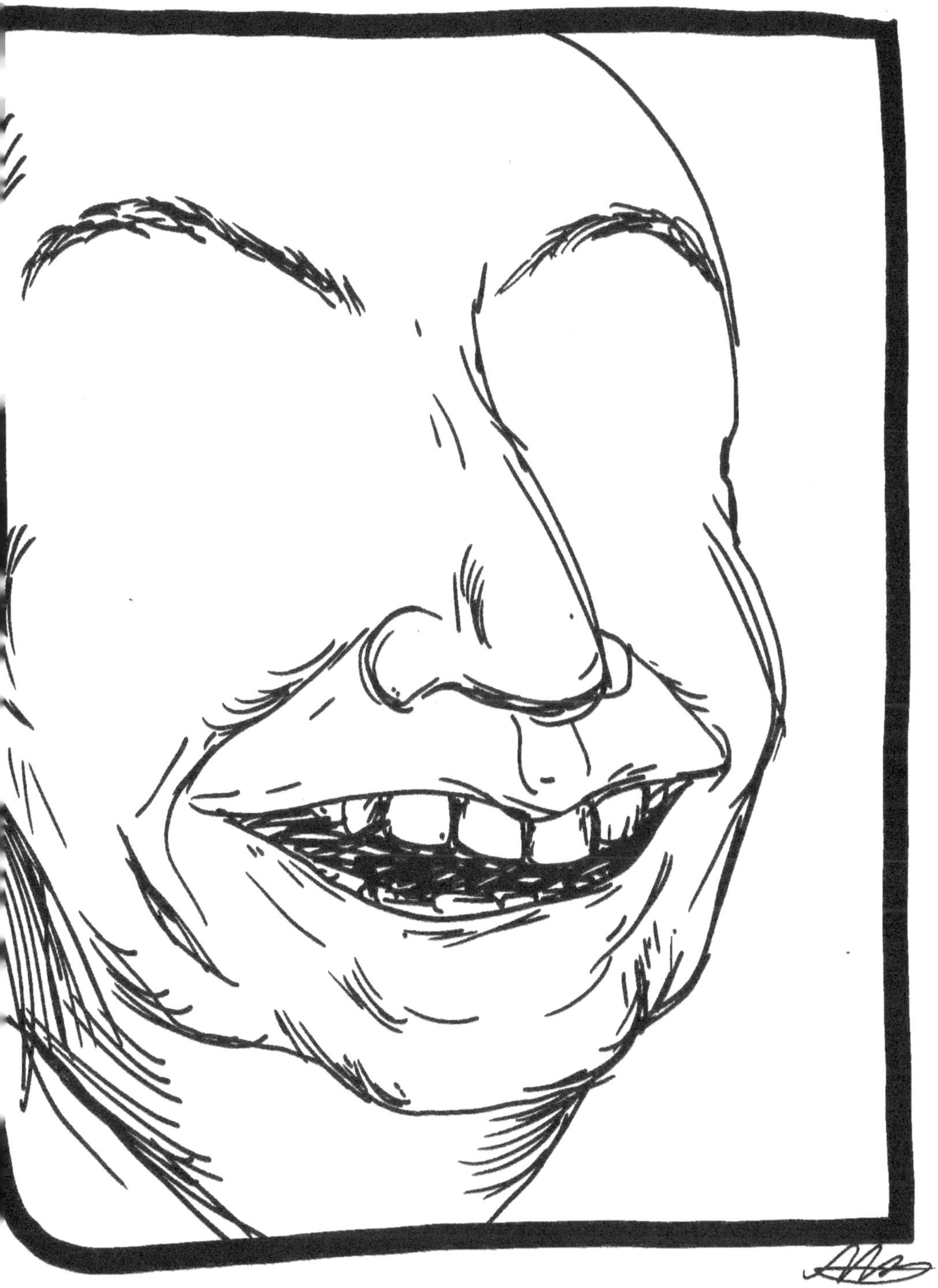

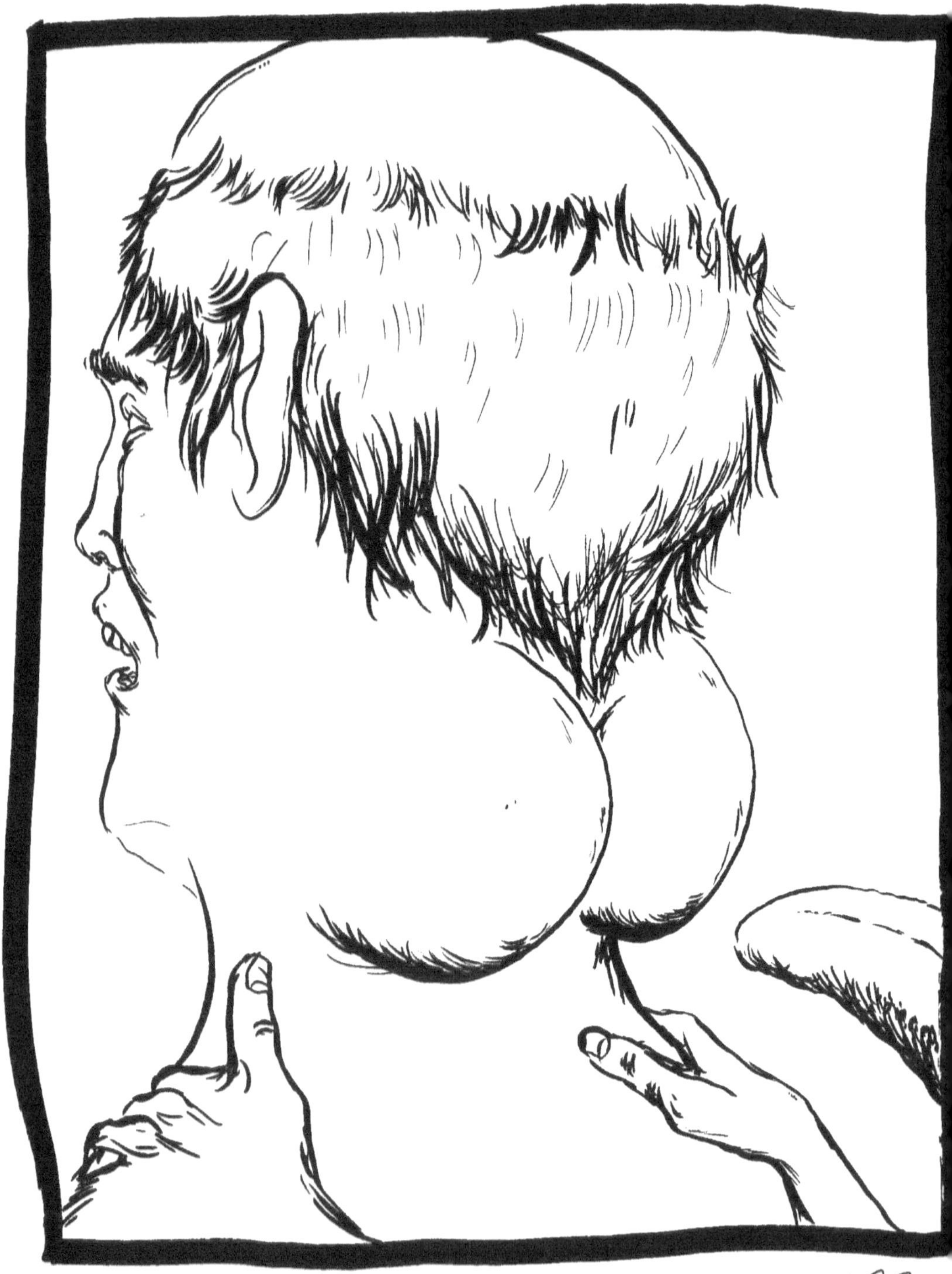

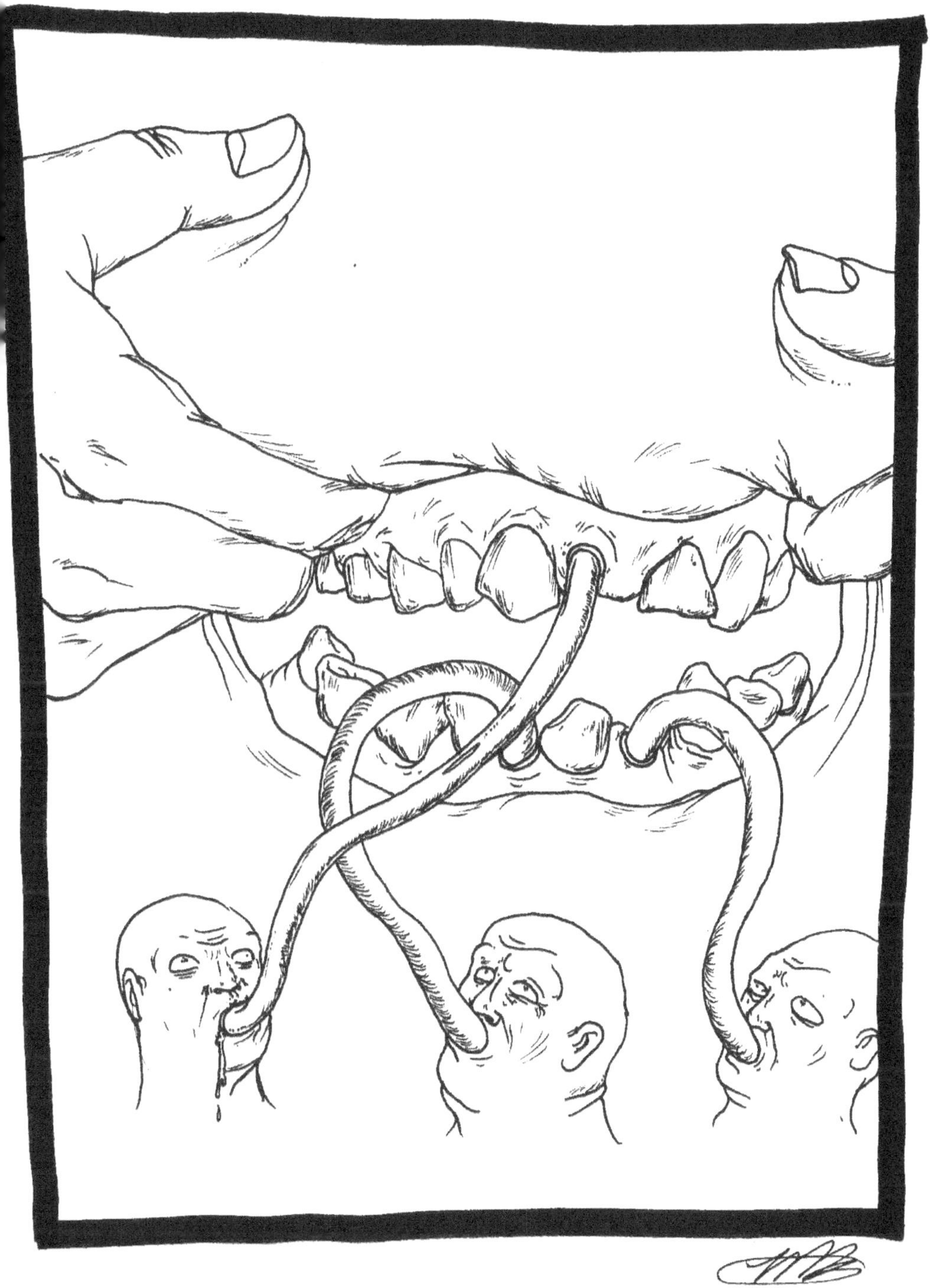

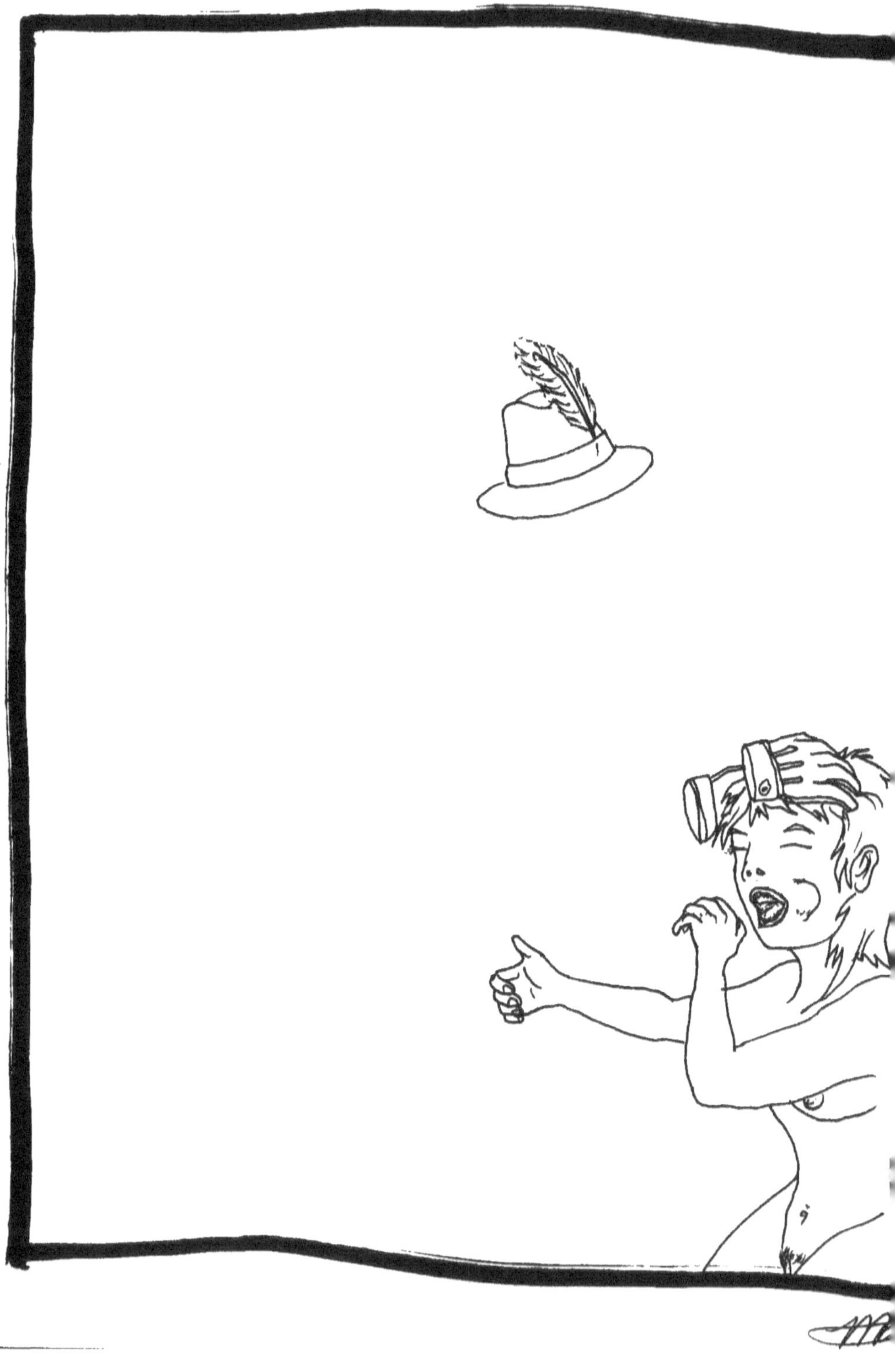

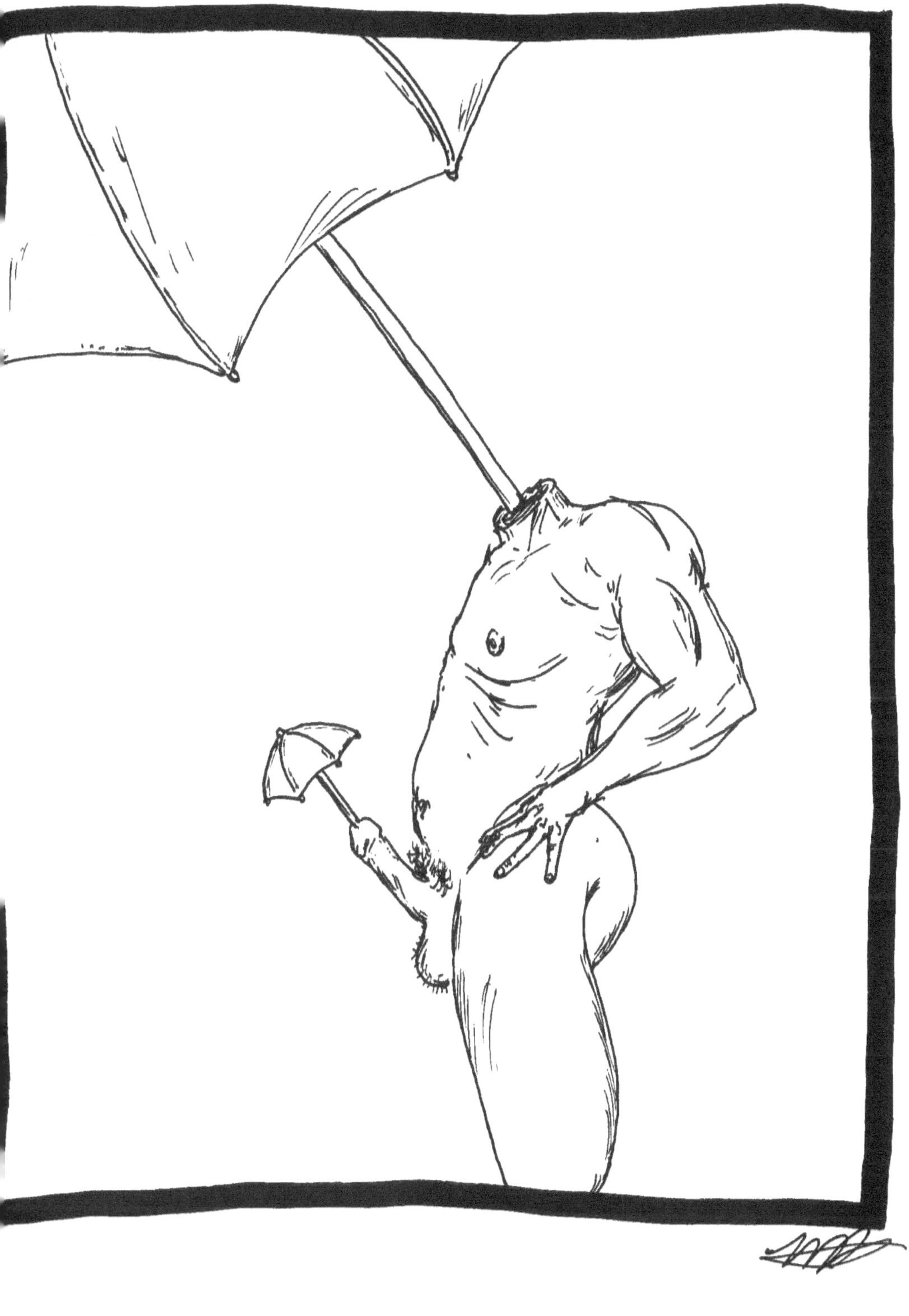

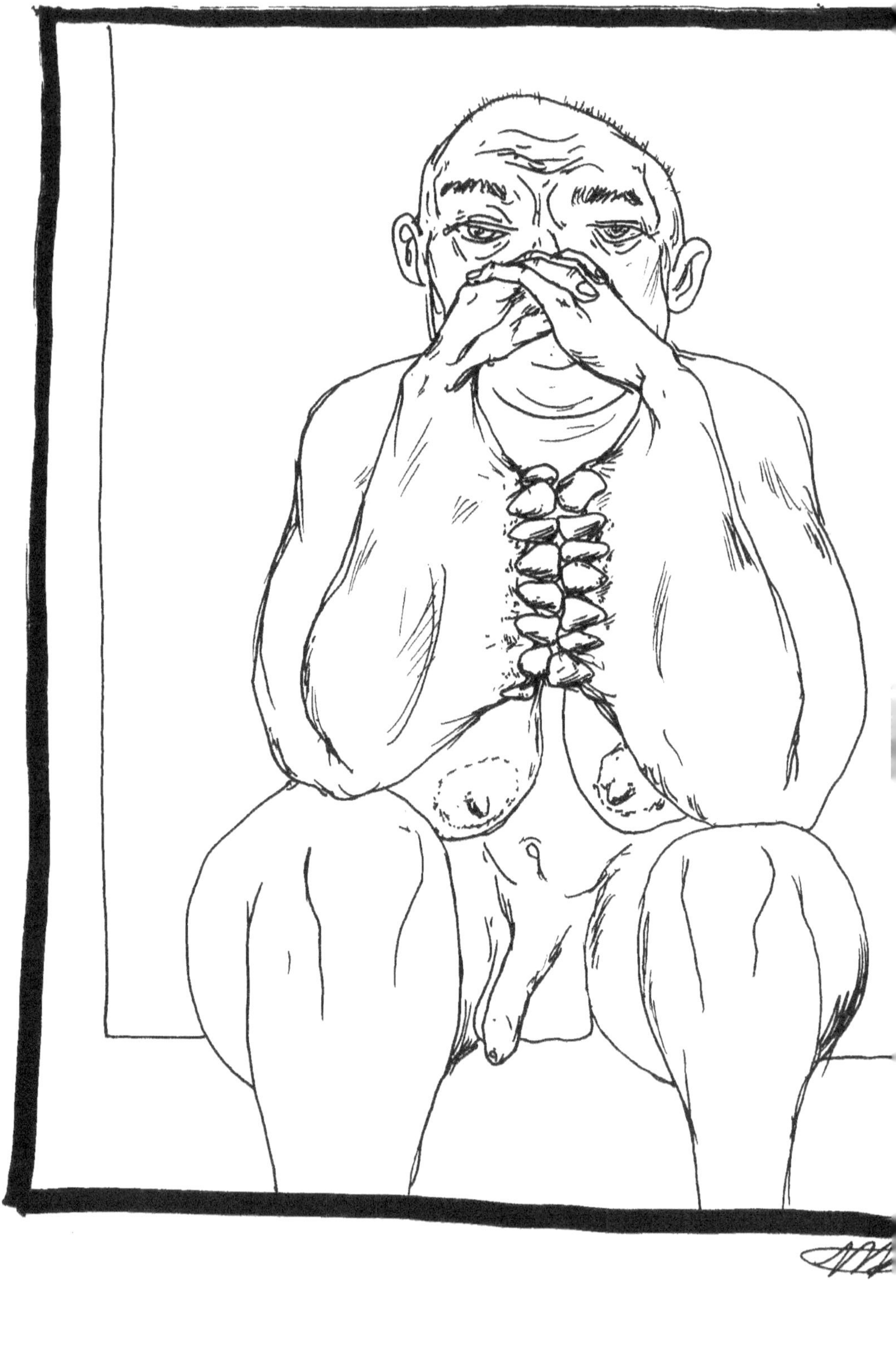

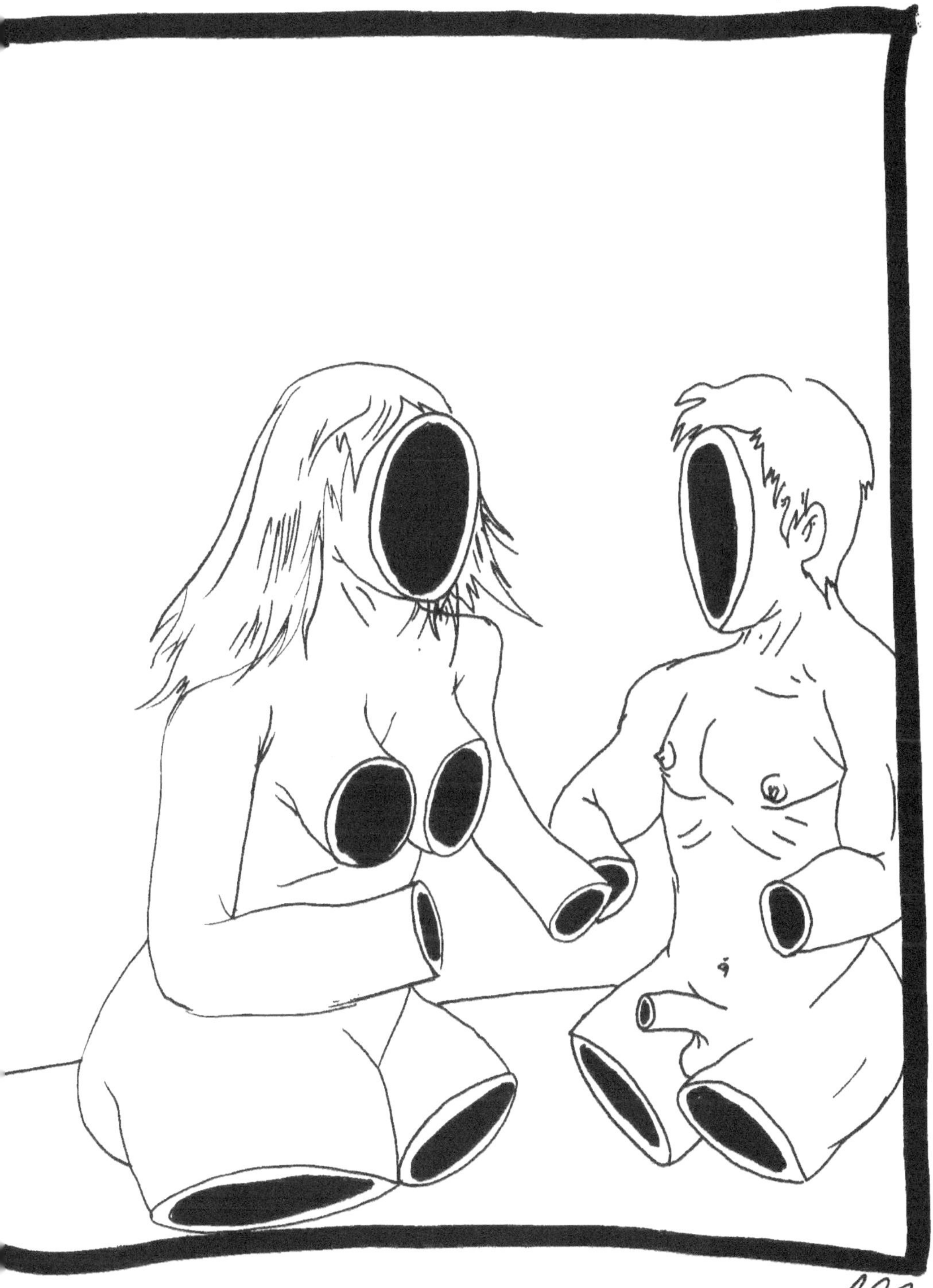

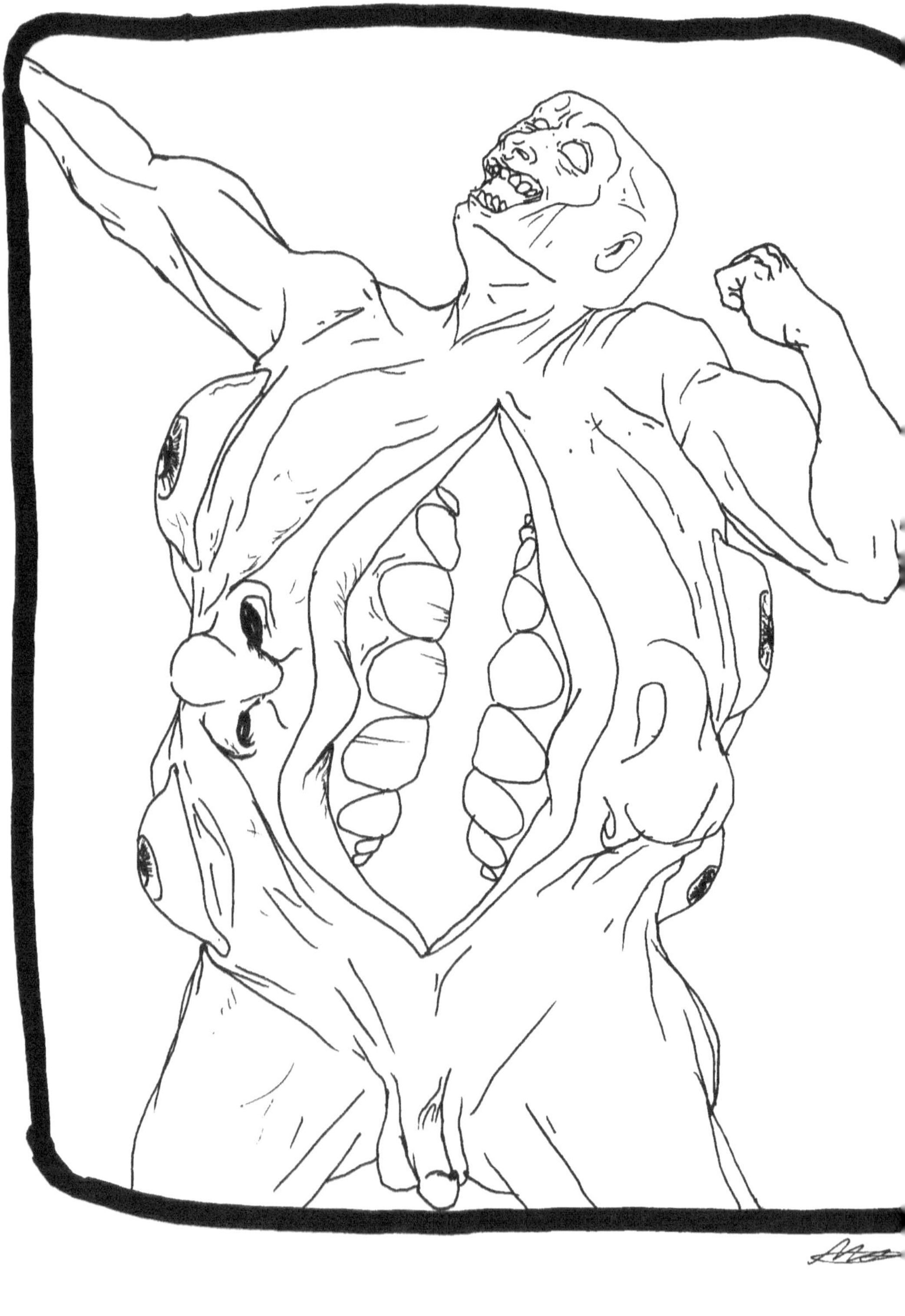

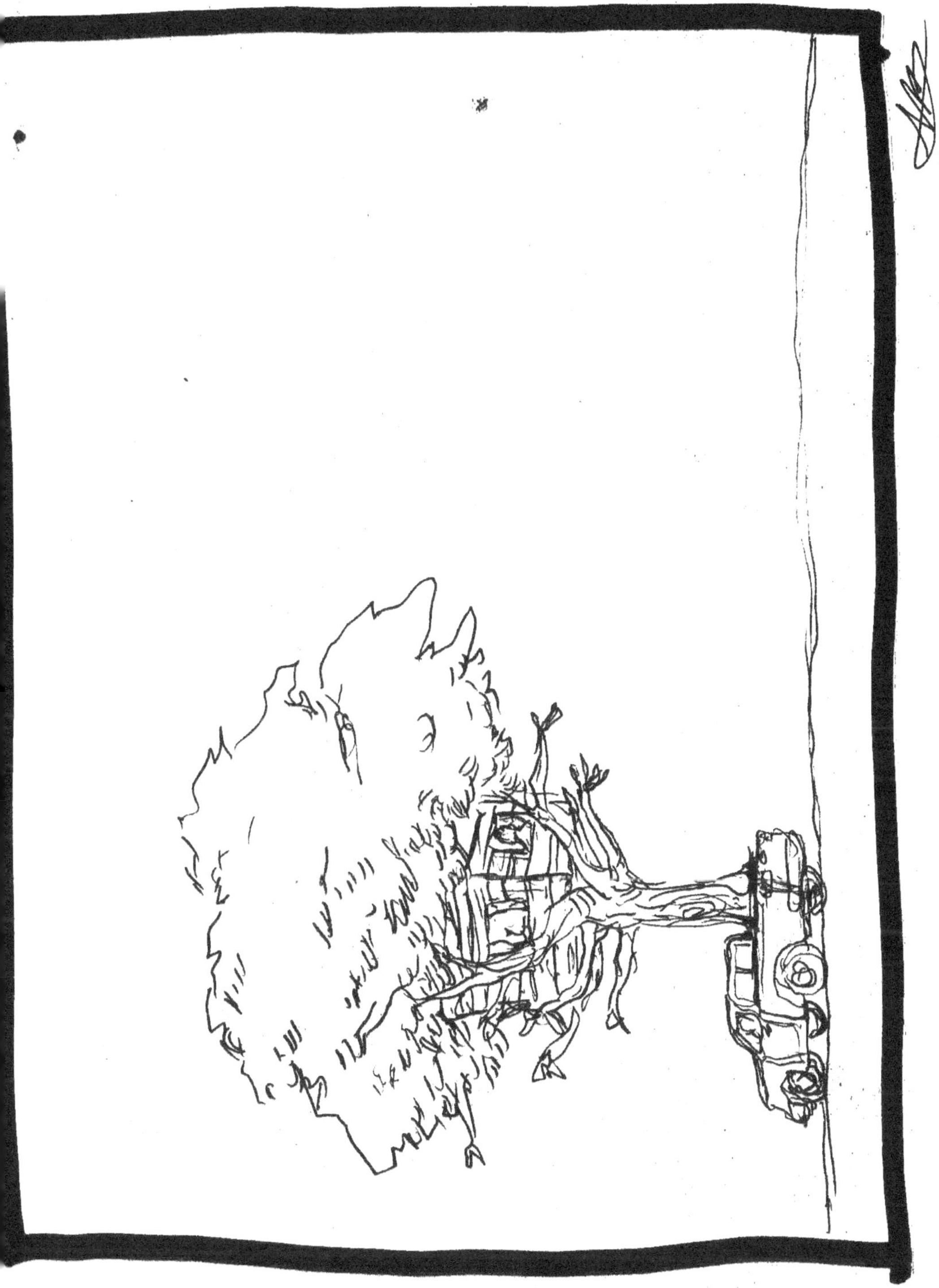

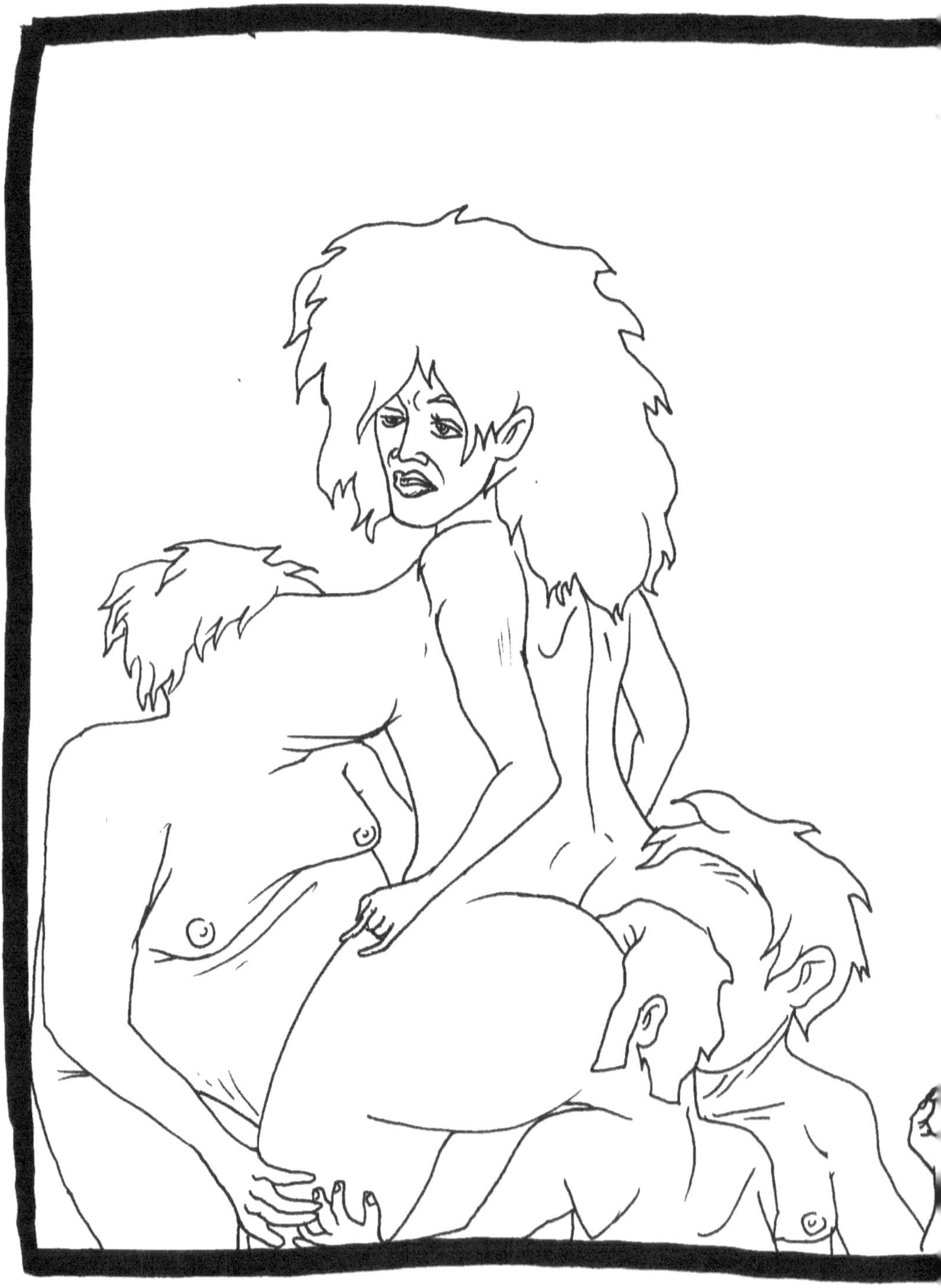

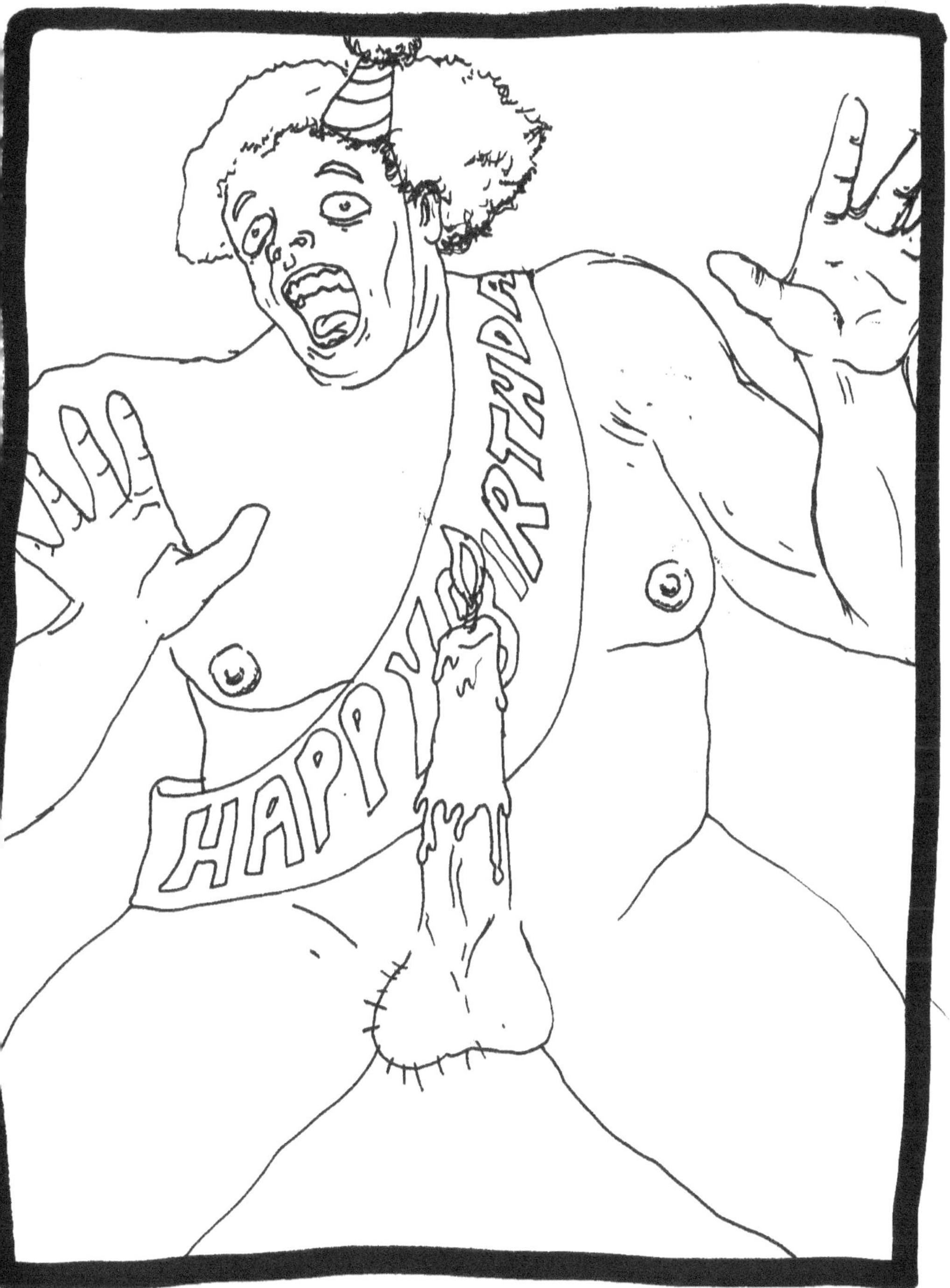
HAPPY
IRTHDA

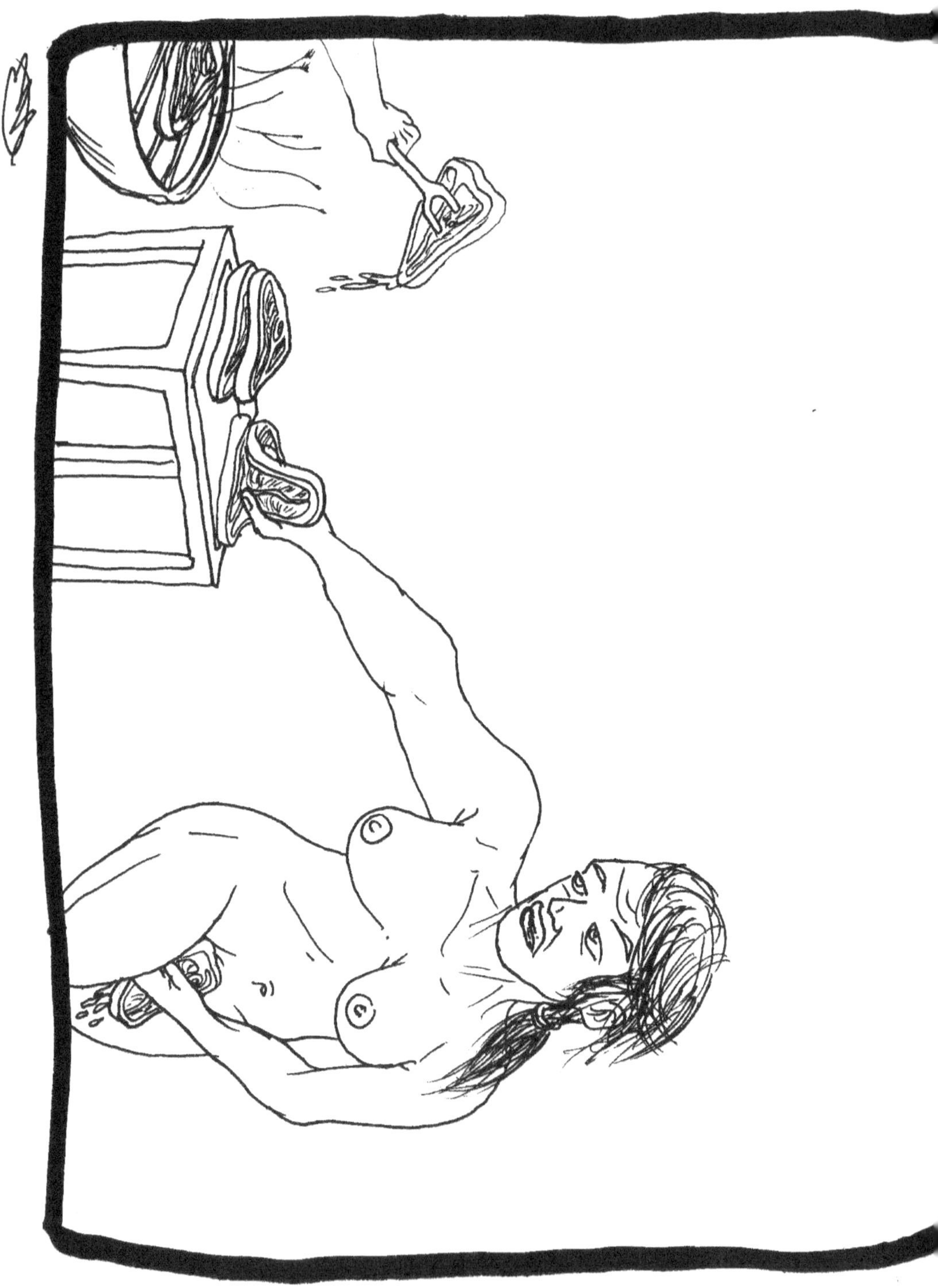

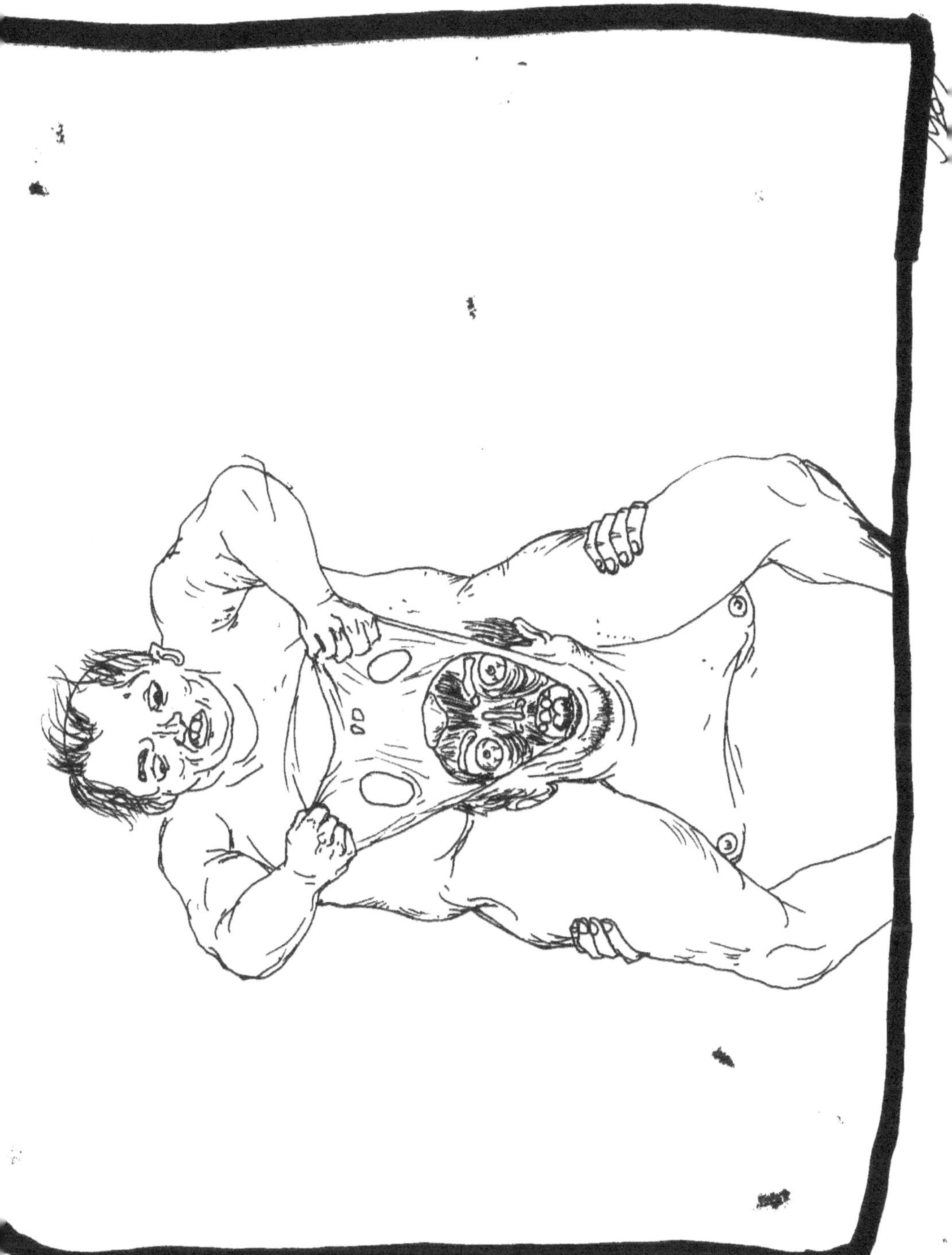

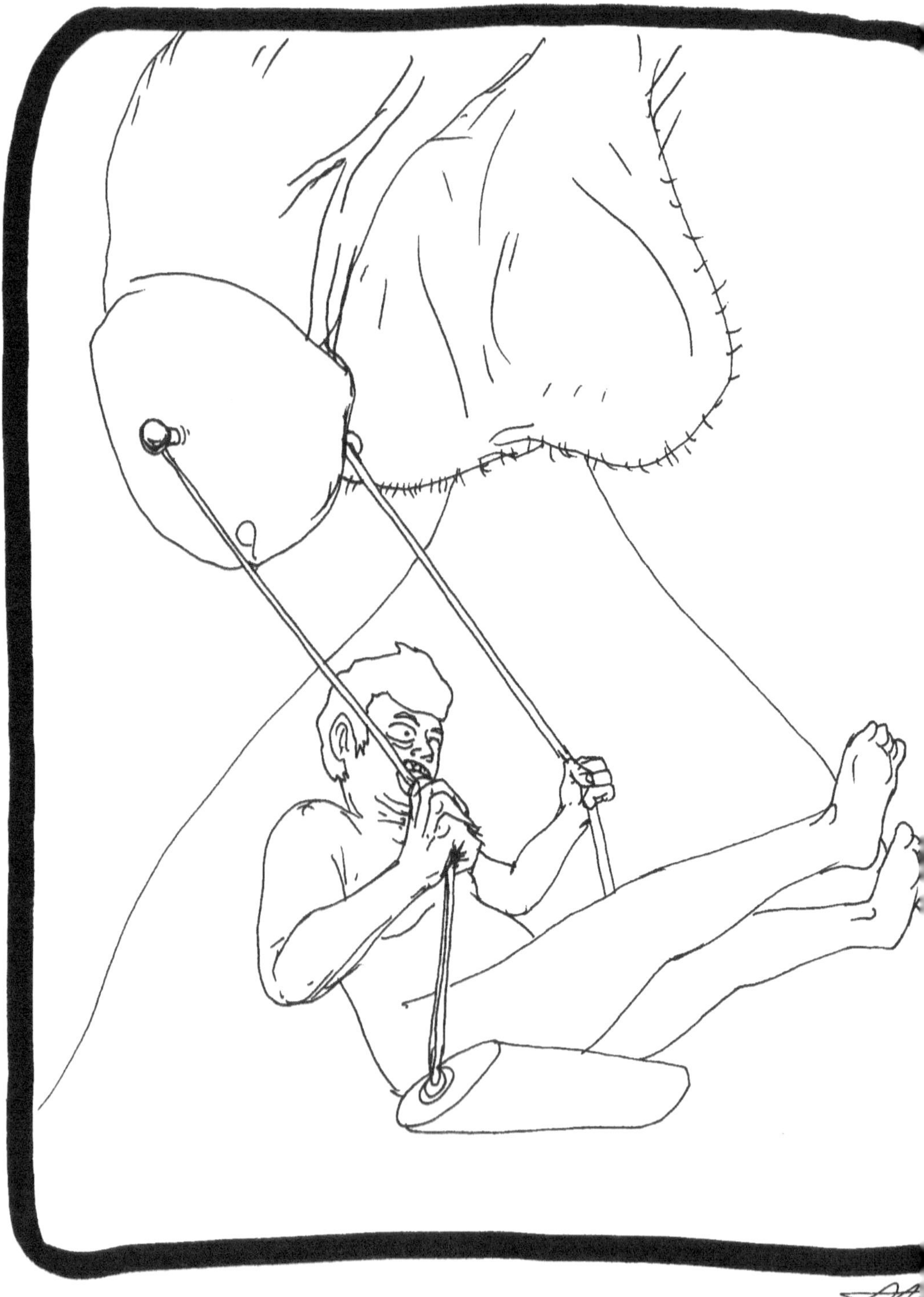

www.ingramcontent.com/pod-product-compliance
Lightning Source LLC
Chambersburg PA
CBHW022109170526
45157CB00004B/1556
* 9 7 8 1 3 2 9 4 4 1 4 0 8 *